LONG TIME COMING

It's been a long, a long time coming
But I know a change is gonna come, oh yes it will

LONG TIME COMING

SHORT WRITINGS FROM ZIMBABWE

edited by
Jane Morris

'amaBooks

ISBN 978-0-7974-3644-2
EAN 9780797436442

Published by 'amaBooks
P.O. Box AC1066, Ascot, Bulawayo
email: amabooks@gator.co.zw
www.amabooksbyo.com

Typeset by 'amaBooks
Printed by Automation Business Forms, Bulawayo

Cover Painting: Charles Nkomo
Cover Design: Veena Bhana

'amaBooks would like to express their thanks to HIVOS and the
Zimbabwe Culture Trust Fund for making this publication possible, and
to Alliance Française de Bulawayo for continuing support.

CONTENTS

ARRESTED DEVELOPMENT

Sandisile Tshuma

I have been standing at Max's Garage for almost three hours trying to hitch a ride to Beitbridge. I am not the only one here though; there must be at least fifty people, maybe even a hundred. Or more, I don't know, whatever; it's hot and I am tired. The point is there is a sizeable crowd of would-be travellers with things to do and places to be and we are all waiting. Desperately. So much about life here and now entails waiting. If you are serious about life, if you are a go-getter and you want to make things happen then you need to know how to wait. Seriously. You take a deep breath, put your 'game face' on, brace yourself and wait. I had to wait two hours to get money from the bank to pay for my journey and now here I am waiting. Again. It's what we do. We wait for transport, for electricity, for rain, for slow-speed internet connections at dingy cyber-cafes in town where we check our mail to see if a nifty little website has found us a job in Dubai or a scholarship to an obscure foreign university, or anything really to get us out of here. And there is never anything, mind you, but you know how hope is. It never dies. So we tell ourselves that there isn't anything *yet*. We'll find a way out; in the meantime let's wait. If you are serious about your life, about surviving, about the future, then you sow some seeds, invest in yourself and you wait. It's my favourite oxymoron, *arrested development*.

I am not hard to spot in this crowd at the barely functioning filling station. I am the sore-thumb of a twenty-something year old woman wearing high-end sunglasses and trendy jeans, carrying minimal luggage and standing in a statuesque pose that is supposed to convince motorists that I would be great company on a major road trip so they should stop for me. I have been here for

1

three hours so clearly something is not working. Maybe they can tell that behind the cool-as-a-cucumber façade of togetherness I am trying to portray is a quivering, fearful little girl who is just dying for someone to take her by the hand and help her cross a busy road. People around me have started grumbling that it's not fair that there are so many cars going to Esigodini but nothing going to Beitbridge or even Gwanda. They are right. No one seems to be going as far as Beitbridge and the longer I stand here the more asinine I feel for thinking that I could do an entire research project on border jumpers in just one lousy weekend. Today is Friday, this thing is due on Tuesday and I can't get out to the field! Why border jumpers anyway? Why did I have to pick a topic that would lead me to the edge of the country? Why not something local like the pipe dream that is the Matabeleland Zambezi Water Pipeline? Well I suppose that's not really local either; besides, it's too controversial. But why do I always procrastinate until there is no time and so much pressure? What is the matter with me?

My internal conversation is interrupted by the sudden realisation that there is a car right in front of me and a swarm of people around me all jostling to get in. *Beitbridge!* I hear someone yell before I am painfully elbowed to the side by a tiny old woman with a rabid look in her eye. Okay this is it. There is no way I am not getting this ride. The driver obviously stopped for me having been won over by my enigmatic side-of-the-road persona, so if these people think they can rob me of my place then they had better think again. It's a double cab and the only space left is right at the back. This is where all those years of compulsory sports at school come in handy. In one deft move I hoist myself into the back sparing a fleeting thought of gratitude to whoever invented stretch denim. Meanwhile women in chiffon blouses and pencil skirts struggle to clamber in with as much dignity as can be achieved while trying not to expose their nether regions to the whole world. Eventually the back is full and we all look at each other with relieved but slightly sheepish smiles in acknowledgement of the elbowing, pushing and shoving it took to get in. There is a word for what we've just done, *Vigoroni*: getting ahead of the crowd and on top of the pile. *Vigo* for short; that's what all the cool people say. It is a brutish, dangerous, undignified must-have skill if you are serious about life and you are a go-getter. You need to know how to wait and when opportunity arrives you need to master the *Vigo*. We are packed like sardines in the searing noon-day sun but we are happy sardines with things to do and places to be and we're off!

Two kilometres down the road the car stops and the driver gets out to collect our fares: eight hundred thousand dollars to Beitbridge. Whatever, prices are so crazy nowadays that I don't even know if that's reasonable or not. I have a feeling it's not and the other passengers don't seem to be comfortable with it either, but it is not in the nature of a Zimbabwean to question or complain. Besides, this is a private car and the owner probably had to get his fuel off the black market so he will offer his service at whatever price the market can bear. There is no public transport, hence we the market are extremely desperate so we wince and bear it. The car does a U-turn and we assume he is going to get some petrol but we find ourselves back at Max's Garage, where the driver tells us that he has changed his mind and will no longer be going to Beitbridge, something to do with the money not covering his fuel costs blah, blah, blah. The others try to convince him to change his mind but at this point I am simply not interested. Just give me my money back, I hiss. He gives me my refund of eight hundred thousand dollars in ten thousand dollar notes and I am not impressed. Great, so here I am a certified waiter and champion of the *Vigo*, defeated. I'm not even trying to look cool anymore. Dear God, please let me get there today. This project is the last hurdle I must clear before I get my qualification in disaster management. Whatever that is. I am commiserating my misery when a young man with a runny nose walks up to me and asks if I'm going to Beitbridge because there is space in the van across the road and it's leaving now. Favour! This is why I am a believer. So I cross the road and get into the front of the van next to a woman in her mid-thirties and then we are well and truly off.

The woman and the driver are talkers, which works perfectly for me because I am a listener, so all I have to do is insert sporadic questions and appropriate exclamations here and there and they do all the work. About ten kilometres down the road we are stopped at a roadblock and the driver has to pay a fine. While he is talking to the traffic officer I get a text message on my mobile phone. It's my friend Lihle who is in Harare. She says that since life expectancy in Zim is reportedly quite low she reckons she is entitled to a mid-life crisis round about now. She obviously has no idea just how low it is. Since it is actually around thirty-seven it is technically too late for a mid-life crisis. *Sori m8. In mid-20s nw so u hav abt 10 mo yrs left 2 liv. Thz r the sunset yrs. 2 18 4 crisis L.* In another place and time, this phase would have been called the quarter-life crisis, during which you are trying to find a balance between fitting into the societal image of responsible adulthood and discovering and doing the things you really want. Like getting a nine-to-five, getting married and having two point four children called Memory, Beauty and Blessing

3

versus pursuing a career in theatre no matter how poorly remunerated it is because that's what makes you feel alive and significant.

The driver is back; he claims he had to pay the police to give him a ticket because he says that this way they won't be able to give him any more tickets at subsequent roadblocks along the way. Okay, I am not even going to try and understand the reasoning involved. So we are off again. It turns out that these two have something in common. They carry contraband between Zimbabwe and South Africa. He is a *Malayitsha*, which means he carries groceries and property sent by Zimbabweans working in South Africa to their families back home. Then on the return leg he carries people: a couple of hundred rand if you have a passport, a couple of thousand if you don't. Business is brisk and he is making a decent living. He can afford to send his three children to good boarding schools, has a great homestead in the communal areas and just bought a property in Bulawayo. She is not to be outdone though. Her contraband of choice is cigarettes: good quality, highly sought after Zimbabwean cigarettes, and she is raking in fifty thousand rand a run. Fifty thousand rand! The drink I was sipping goes down the wrong tube and I am spluttering and coughing, trying very hard to regain my composure and not look like the naïve good little citizen that I am.

My pulse is racing. Life is hard, she says, but for her life has never been better. She has a townhouse in Johannesburg, one in Pumula and is building in Mahatshula and Selborne Park. There is something about Bulawayo, she says. While she is talking I rattle off the figures in my mind. Fifty thousand rand a run! How many runs a month? How much to pay off the cops? And the insider at customs? And who are her buyers? What is the initial investment outlay? Girlfriend, what are you still doing at school? There is money to be made in hard currency! Then it occurs to me that she could be one of these *nouveau riche* types a friend of mine was complaining about some time ago. They buy grotesquely oversized mock Victorian style furniture that is obscenely expensive and fill their homes with high tech gadgets they never use and very expensive but distastefully generic art. I remember him agonising *Like, hello! They don't even know a Tamuka Mtetwa from an Eric Gauss!* I frown, unsure that I know the difference either. But I feel his bitterness! She is going on about how she dropped out of high school and does not regret it. It is official, I am bitter. *Wow,* I say feigning nonchalance; *you must really shop up a storm at Fort 11 flea market.* She squeals delightedly, not sensing my sarcasm, *Yes!* Then she launches into a long tirade about how she never buys authentic designer labels and she would much rather buy a thousand pairs of cheap shoes made in Korea. Yup, she is indeed one of them I decide, before sinking deeper into the car seat feeling like an inadequate non-achiever. I'll take my mid-life crisis now if you don't mind: shaken, not stirred. Whatever.

In Gwanda we pick up someone to sit in the back of the van. He speaks some type of hybrid Zulu with a heavy Shona accent. The driver disappears for a good twenty minutes during which the newcomer too has a story to tell. He works in Johannesburg and came home two weeks ago for a relative's funeral in Marondera. In Beitbridge the transport situation was so bad that he had to wait eighteen hours for a mini-bus to fill up with enough people to make the trip to Bulawayo viable. He decided to change his rands to local currency with some young men who offered him a good exchange rate. Not having been in the country for a few years he was unfamiliar with the new currency. They gave him a couple of thousand dollars in $100 and $500 notes in exchange for eight hundred rand in hard earned cash. Unbelievable! I am mortified on his behalf. Did he not count the money? That amount should have earned him over twenty million dollars on the black market. *They said something about slashing zeros,* he recalls with a rueful smile. The woman, who has introduced herself as Gloria, seems to find the story immensely amusing. *Ha! They really got you, my friend! You know that was the equivalent of twenty rand, which means you just gave them seven hundred and eighty rand! Ha! Ha! They really got you. I'll bet they were Shona. Those are the only crooks in Beitbridge, unlike the Ndebele who are too lazy and us Vendas who make an honest hustle.* Completely dumbstruck by her blatant tribalism, I look at the young man who is very obviously Shona, to study his reaction to what I perceive to be a total lack of empathy on Gloria's part. Poor chap; he is taking it like a trooper. *Yes, my sister, they really got me. I had to sell my phone to raise money to come back.* Gloria throws her head back laughing. *Never trust a Shona! Never trust a woman either! Trust no one, not even your relatives. We are all trying to survive here and if you are not alert it is only the fool who won't take advantage.* I am furious with her for her attitude but at the same time she is hard to dislike. She has the type of gritty raw honesty that does nothing for a person's self esteem but makes one see the truth in all its cruelty. And that is what makes one toughen up. This chap, having been ridiculed this way, will never be conned again. The driver returns and the conversation ends as the journey resumes.

I am gazing out the window watching the world go by, or rather is it the world that watches me pass by? Somewhere behind me the sun sets over

5

Zimbabwe. This day, like so many other things in my country, is slipping into the arms of the past. As the kilometres go by I am struck by a loneliness that I have noticed in everyone lately. It is a pervasive and virus-like affliction that insinuates itself into every public social gathering and intimate lovers' embrace. It comes in waves that bear transcendental glimpses of what once was: a life and future that existed briefly in the collective consciousness of twelve million people and we can feel it slipping through our fingers. All we can do is watch helplessly. Or can we?

The driver and Gloria are in an animated discussion about the dangers of their trades. They talk of payment defaulters being sold off to Nigerians in Johannesburg, strip searches and muggings by bandits in the farmlands of Limpopo Province, swimming across the Limpopo and hoping that if there must be a crocodile attack let it be the person next to you that is eaten because you really need this to work out. They talk of paying off border officials, highway police, farmers, magistrates, anyone and everyone. There isn't a palm that can't be greased, apparently. But surely there are some palms that you cannot bring yourself to grease, either because they are already so dirty that you are afraid some of it will come off on you, or because no one else has ever dared to grease them. It is just getting dark when we arrive at the busy border town. Gloria curses as she realizes that she forgot her passport and she's supposed to be collecting some money at the South African border town of Musina tomorrow. No worries though, she knows a guy who can organize a gate pass for her at a small fee. Another text message from Lihle who reckons her bride price has at least quadrupled since she came to Zimbabwe from the UK to get her study visa. *I am such a catch! I'm intelligent, educated and beautiful, I can fetch water, light a fire and cook a decent meal and I can find anything in the dark.* It is good to see she has found something positive about these endless power cuts. A few weeks ago she was upset because her expensive imported hairpiece always smells like wood smoke...

Saying my goodbyes to my travel-mates I step out of the car and inhale deeply the warm, dusty air. I came here for statistics and figures on irregular migrants but these figures have names and faces. They include seasoned smooth operators of the system like Gloria and clueless teens fresh out of high school in the rural areas that are carried by *Malayitshas* and are easy fodder for unscrupulous people on either side of the border. They are go-getters who are desperately serious about life and, as I walk into the starry night, I hope I can do them justice.

THE AWARDS CEREMONY

John Eppel

Two patriots, a glorious son and a glorious daughter, were to be honoured this sunny late-winter day, July 28, 2007. They were to receive Zimbabwe's second highest civilian merit award: the Tupperware Cross (rust-free, water-resistant, available only at the most respectable retail outlets). And there to pin the medals on his chest and her breast (I'll fumble this one) was none other than the Deputy Minister of Borrowdale Shopping Centre, Comrade Colonel Bolo d'Ingati-Swatibumbum.

The venue was the Large City Hall in Bulawayo, and it was packed to crumbling capacity. The atmosphere was thick with anticipation and the reek of chicken and chips fried in rancid oil. The recipients sat demurely in the front row watching the entertainment that preceded the awards ceremony. Even from my cramped position near the back, I could make out that both recipients were in uniform: hers of the nursing profession, and his of the police force. What added to the glamour of the occasion was the indisputable fact that they were a married couple. I had to crane my neck to see that they were actually holding hands.

The proceedings were only two hours late, yet the entertainers were flagged. What could you expect of ten year old girls, clearly malnourished, wearing the skimpiest costumes, and having to keep up with the man who played the *isigubhu* and who doubled (or should I say trebled) as their manager and as tonight's master of ceremonies. He was magnificently arrayed in a leopard skin and a pair of unmistakably *Calvin Klein* underpants. (I mention these child entertainers because of the tragedy that befalls them in the closing minutes of the ceremony.)

7

Meanwhile they gyrated their skinny, pre-pubertal bodies in the most suggestive of ways before an audience that was, by contrast, obese – a sure sign that they were paid-up members of the ruling party. One woman was wearing a blouse the size of a double-bed sheet, which sported the slogan: OUR PRESIDENT FOR LIFE. There were slogans on shirts, dresses, and even trousers all over the hall: PASI ne BLAIR, PASI ne BUSH, PASI ne PIOUS; PAMBERI ne ZANU-PF, PAMBERI ne CHIMURENGA THREE, PAMBERI ne GRAIN MARKETING BOARD; NO VACANCIES WITHIN THE PRESIDIUM; FORWARD WITH OPERATION DZIKISA MITENGO....

At last, the Minister made his appearance, not, initially, on stage, but accompanying his enormous wife in the separate compartment, known as a box, which is reserved for dignitaries. It is located near the ceiling, stage left, and juts out from the wall like a balcony. The chairs in the box had to be replaced by a large settee in order to accommodate the pretty giantess. She was holding a *Kentucky Fried* drumstick in one hand, and a glass of *Coca Cola* in the other. She was wearing a crimson velvet dress, which might once have been stage curtains.

Heads and television cameras swivelled to the right and tilted at an angle of seventy degrees. Feet stamped, hands clapped, tongues ululated, and lips whistled. The guest of honour, resplendent in his bemedalled (sic) army uniform, gave us a smart salute, and proceeded, circuitously, to the stage, where he made an hour-long speech condemning those proxies of Blair and Bush who were working with unpatriotic elements to undermine the great and glorious gains of the liberation struggle. He brought down the house with some scurrilous comments about a certain Archbishop (name supplied), and then went into top gear churning out what people even higher than he in the ranks of power churned out: "The fight against Zimbabwe [he was now reading, somewhat hesitantly, from a script] is the fight against us all. Today it is Zimbabwe, tomorrow it will be South [er] Africa... it will be Mozambique... it will be Angola... it will be any oth [er] African country. And any gov [er] nment that is p [er] ceived to be strong, and to be resistant to imp [er] ialists, will be made a target and will be und [er] mined. So let us not allow any point of weakness in the sol [er] darity of the SADC, because that weakness will also be transf [er] red to the rest of Africa." He used the phrase 'sov [er] eign state' no fewer than sixteen times in the course of his diatribe. The audience adored him.

Finally he turned to the purpose of this gathering of party faithful (don't

8

ask me, *mon semblable, mon frère*, what I was doing there) and called the hero and the heroine to the stage. Both kept their heads modestly bowed as they gathered in a comradely fashion on either side of that beautifully pressed uniform with its tinkling medals. Both recipients of the award had shown extreme patriotism in the execution of their duties. By strangling five terminally ill patients at Bulawayo's Ububele Hospital, Comrade Sister Chigaramanhenga had helped to solve the problem of urban overcrowding, in the spirit of the by no means exhausted government initiative, Operation Murambatsvina (clear out the human excrement). By beating so severely, with a metre long rubberized truncheon, and by stomping so energetically with his size twelve hob-nailed boots, seven women supporters of the National Constitutional Assembly, that they later died of their injuries, Comrade Inspector Chigaramanhenga had helped preserve his country's sovereignty in its struggle against Western-backed advocates of regime-change, like whites, coloureds, Indians, and... er... Ndebeles. The fact that the seven women, two of them expectant mothers, had all been Shona did not seem relevant in the present circumstances.

Then he pinned the medals, first on the police officer, who responded with a smart salute, then (much fumbling here) on the nursing sister, who responded with a delicate curtsey. The audience exploded, and that energy, combined with ministerial bulk (the wife), dislodged the VIP box, and it came crashing down onto the little girls who had danced for us to the point of exhaustion. They had been made to stand under the box in order to watch the awards ceremony. All six were killed instantly, but the Minister's wife bounced into safety, calling out "Where's my tub of *Kentucky Fried*?"

9

BUS FARE

Julius Chingono

My brother could not be located. At his place of work, he could not be found. The security guard at the main gate was not sure that he'd seen him that morning when everybody arrived for work. The receptionist said that there was no reply from his office. The girl at the switchboard could not reach him and the workshop hauler got no response, yet some of his workmates claimed that they'd seen him and talked to him earlier that day. I was tempted to enquire at the personnel office, but I hesitated because I was not sure whether he was officially away from work or had just slipped away without permission. To raise the issue of his whereabouts might perhaps give him away. So I waited outside at the gate, praying that he was in the factory somewhere. I had no bus fare to take me home and the time was 4.45 pm. The factory would close for the day in fifteen minutes and the workers would soon be streaming out. I paced up and down trying to figure out alternative means of finding transport back home – twenty kilometres away, at St Mary's township in Chitungwiza.

Now I was in Graniteside industrial area. Walking back home would be an effort. Besides, the road between Harare and Chitungwiza was impossible to travel at night because of the many highway robbers. The tall grass, thick bush and trees between Hatfield and Manyame Bridge were intimidating and the highway that serviced the two towns had no lights. Even motorists feared to venture down this road late at night. I was sure I would not reach home safely if I relied on my feet. And there was no potential benefactor to offer me bus fare other than my brother in Graniteside. I knew he would definitely find me the five thousand dollars from his workmates if he did not have money on him. He would not desert me, having often bailed me out of financial problems, big or small. I asked myself if the security guard was conducting his duties properly. Surely he was posted at the gate to check who went in and out. How could he afford to be so unsure of my brother's whereabouts?

My eyes kept vigil as I paced slowly along the fence near the gate. Delivery trucks bumped back into the factory yard. Small vehicles and motorbikes drove in fast. And the first batch of tired workers exited and hurried to the bus stop a hundred metres away. I saw money change hands. I wished I were on the receiving end. I heard someone shout, "By 5.30 I will be drinking my first mug of beer." Suddenly there was a deluge of men in overalls and work suits at the gate and the ancillary road. Industrial clank and cacophony was transferred to the roads where traffic hummed, braked and honked. The voices of excited pedestrians going home dominated the roads. I wished I were one of them, going home to a mug of opaque beer. What was beer when I did not have money for bus fare? I scowled as I came to stand at the gate.

"Old man, we do not allow strangers to stand in front of this gate. How many times must I tell you?" The security guard shouted at me and showed me where to wait, across the road. I wanted to wait right at the gate because I wanted to make sure I saw every person who came out through the exit. So I walked across the road grudgingly and waited until there seemed to be no one left in the factory. The security guard seemed to enjoy my vigil as the last of the managers' smart vehicles drove out. Peering. Bending. I lost hope.

"By the way, *mudhara*, you said you wanted to see... who... Noboth... your brother?" the security guard asked, walking towards me across the road. He stood akimbo before me and waited for me to respond. He was now relaxed because the company managers had left. He was now free to loiter.

"Yes," I replied resignedly.

"I think er – e – e – I saw him walk out the gate... I remember... it was at tea break." He stretched his body and hands and yawned noisily.

"And you saw him come back?" I was beginning to doubt his memory. His renewed efforts did not impress me. He was only trying to find someone to chat with until it was time for him to go home.

"I heard him shout back to his workmates... it was something to do with collecting his ID at the Registrar General's offices in town." For the first time he sounded sure of his words. He walked slowly back to the gate.

"But why didn't you tell me before?" My shout sounded like that of an angry, hopeless child.

11

"That is not my job, *mudhara*. Moreover heavy traffic comes in and out through this gate. I cannot remember everything that happens... unless it's recorded in my log book here." He took a big black book that was on a platform of bricks. He tried to show me how he made entries in it but I abruptly turned and walked away. I sensed he was one clever person trying to find company. Delaying me with his paperback tactics.

I walked, not exactly knowing where I was going, without even realising that the road I was taking took me even further away from home. I walked hopelessly. Julius Nyerere Way. Jason Moyo. Leopold Takawira Street. Samora Machel Avenue. First Street. I was on automatic drive. I longed to meet someone I knew. I met no one. The November sun was setting fast like it was already 6.45 pm.

I was turning aimlessly from George Silundika Avenue into Angwa Street when I heard a female voice call, "Baba vaFaith! Baba vaFeyi!" The voice sounded familiar. I immediately gave it my undivided attention and my tired body jerked with inflated expectation. The voice was a blessing, the voice of a person who really knew me, a person who even knew the name of my daughter. I was glad I had stumbled upon someone I knew. Now things would turn out all right. Whoever she was, she was going to bail me out. I would certainly ask her to give me money for bus fare.

The owner of the voice was Amai Faith. She lifted her weight sturdily as she crossed the street from the opposite pavement. She smiled a smile that showed that she knew me well. She strode heavily on the tarmac swaying her body energetically. Her flared skirt swirled up and down her knees. Her sandals clicked on the tarmac. Her naked brown shoulders were exuberant in the glow of sunset. I licked my lips, but they did not seem to respond to the lubricant. I feared they were white and dry. I wished I looked more presentable. I looked into the window of the furniture shop behind me. Amai Faith was half way across the road. My shoes said it all – that I was trying but failing to cover life's dents. They were bursting at the seams, and my shirt was patched. Suddenly my trousers seemed too short, the bottom hem rose way above my ankles. I no longer felt respectable. My hands made a dash for my shoes, my trousers and whatever I could find amiss and straighten up in those few short seconds as she bore down on me. I now regretted that I was meeting someone I was not supposed to meet. I felt awkward even as my chances of getting bus fare drew closer.

Amai Faith, my former wife, shone in the November twilight. She was the same person I had married and lived with many years before. I felt challenged. I put my hands in my pockets and raised my head above my shoulders to emphasise that it, at least, was still above water. By the way my former wife was dressed, life seemed fine for her. I decided I was not prepared to discuss my problems with a previous spouse, let alone mention my need for bus fare. I pretended to be unconcerned. I lent my tired frame against a nearby pillar, smiled and welcomed her, my legs casually crossed.

"I was beginning to think that you'd moved out of Harare," I said, trying to give the impression of nonchalance. The reflective window behind me had warned me not to overdo my act. My teeth had acquired a golden rustic colour. We shook hands. She looked me in the face and I managed to add, "You know how it is these days. Most things in life cannot be relied upon. It is not like the past." Attempting to be philosophical, I tried to dilute the tension of a separation of more than twenty years. Her hands were soft and her facial tone had lightened considerably. Lightening creams, I presumed from the skin that had formed pouches beneath her eyes.

"What could have happened to me...? I'm not adventurous...." She laughed and stood by my side, a position for which I was grateful as I did not have to face her scrutinising eyes. I had married again three years after our separation. She had remained single, with custody of our two children. I had disappeared from her life and that of the children, just as if I'd been in jail. Now two decades later, the past had resurfaced in Angwa Street, and me without bus fare.

"So how are you, Amai Feyi? You have grown more beautiful with age." She blushed and fidgeted with the latch of her leather purse, just like her old self. Sweet, heavy perfume filled my nose. I smiled tightly.

"I'm fine and you?" Her voice was frighteningly soft.

"How are the children?" I hoped I did not sound regretful.

"They're okay.... Feyi is doing her first degree and Fitz is doing his second." She sounded triumphant.

"I knew they'd make it. They'll end up taking care of you." I was not qualified to say as much, although I had been kept well informed by some freelance gossips who breathed the air between me and her.

"They are dying to see you... I do not know when I will introduce them to you." She was apologetic. "They would love to..." I laughed a little, embarrassment playing hip hop with my voice.

"They would love to see me..." I felt awkward. The last time I saw the children was when Faith was four and Fitz was five.

"How is work?" She helpfully changed the subject, but I was lost. How

13

could I find myself being introduced to my children? My eyes fell to the pavement.

"Work?" My exclamation startled her because it was conveyed in a loud voice. I wiped my dusty brow.

"I have been out of work for three years." I wished I hadn't met her. I licked my lips. "Shut-downs, fold-ups, retrenchments. No work."

"It is these sanctions that have done it. At our workplace, the society has ceased staff recruitment." She was the Programme Co-ordinator with the Red Cross. Her service had spanned eighteen years.

Then she continued seamlessly, "You know what, I'm trying to find change for a two hundred thousand dollar note. I need money for bus fare to Parirenyatwa Hospital. Do you have any change?"

How could she ask such a question? Couldn't she see for herself? I did not look like a person who worked. I didn't have a cent on me. I was looking for bus fare. I did not know where I was going to sleep. I avoided the question, "Who is in hospital?"

"My friend's daughter. Come, let's have a drink at the petrol station so I can get some change." She was already lifting her heavy weight along Angwa Street when I consented, "Though I prefer alcohol to *Fanta*."

Not knowing if she had heard or not, I followed as if I was being pulled. I had lost all hope of finding bus fare. The sun had set and the streets were flooded with light. We turned into George Silundika Avenue and then Second Street. I kept to her pace. Silence prevailed. A few people were still plying the streets. A cool wind fanned our faces and I wondered why she had not responded to my aside. Was she still strongly against alcohol? It was my drinking habits that had caused our separation.

"If you could phone me on Tuesday, I will refer you to a friend's husband. He is a manager at a departmental store and, at this time of the year, the store engages temporary staff for Christmas business." She regarded me pointedly as she handed me my choice of drink. The attendant brought her change, a thick wad of thousand dollar notes. My tongue rolled around my lips. I turned my head away and pretended that I was not interested in their transactions. But my mind wished the money was mine.

"I will phone. By the way, what is your number?"

"Zero two three eight nine seven six…" I struggled to remember the last two figures.

"Don't worry, the attendant can help us with a pen." My enthusiasm for her contacting some manager on my behalf was not total. I gulped my drink

14

and nearly choked. I did not want to appear so desperate. I coughed a little and scratched my nose. "He must have something to write with."

To show my appreciation for her effort I leapt forward and loudly requested a pen from the attendant who threw me one to catch. She wrote her number on a used bus ticket. I put the small piece of paper into my shirt pocket.

"In these hard times jobs can be found only through some connection." I finished my drink, pouring it down my throat into my empty stomach. Her tone was light and she was happy that I accepted her offer. She burped contentedly.

"Yhaa a a a." It was a long pitiful sound I ejected, just like a sigh of relief. She looked at me and I hid my face behind the empty bottle in my hand. She handed me her empty bottle to pass on to the attendant. She cocked her head as she tried to find my face, but my face could not be found so easily. My eyes darted from the petrol pump to the attendant, to the deep freeze and the letters written Second Street Service Station. And I found total escape when I took the empty bottles to the attendant. My footsteps made disturbed sounds of uncontrolled speed on a smooth pavement.

"I will have to catch a taxi. It's only fifteen minutes to visiting hour." She peered at her watch and we walked side by side. The cold drink and the cool evening wind made me feel a little more relaxed. One minute I was feeling fine and the next there was this nag, the bus fare. Can I ask her for bus fare? She has the money. She seems to be in a benevolent mood. What if she says the money she has is for the upkeep of the patient she is visiting? I mused as we walked quietly to the taxi rank. But five thousand dollars could not get her off budget. I sighed. She stole a glance at me, which I recognised and dodged. She seemed to have sensed my discomfort. We did not talk until we reached the taxi rank.

Talk, say out your problem, I encouraged myself, but my jaws were heavy and my tongue was stuck. She held the door latch of the taxi she had chosen to hire. She looked at me once more. She did not close the door immediately. "Do not fail to phone. I will have made the necessary arrangements." Her voice was genuine. Julius, ask for bus fare! Five thousand dollars only! Where will you sleep?

"I will." My voice was of an accused taking an oath after pleading. She shut the door. "Parirenyatwa Hospital," she addressed the cab-man. My feet were stuck on the tarmac beside the taxi and I breathed heavily. "Bye, Baba vaFeyi, I will be expecting your call." She smiled.

"Bye bye-e-e." I salvaged some sound. The driver started the engine and engaged first gear. I raised my hopeless hand to wave her goodbye. The taxi drove off.

"Wait, driver...." I heard her voice below the hum of the engine. I saw her hand hold out to me bank notes, accompanied by an affectionate smile. "You can have that for beer, or rather alcohol." She let out a loud chuckle and the taxi sped off. The remnants of her chuckle echoed in my head until I was in full light. I held tight the five twenty thousand dollar notes until I reached the bus station. I counted the money again and again, not believing my unexpected good fortune. Bus fare? And a two litre scud would do me no harm, I said to myself as I started to feel a strong thirst for opaque beer. The overpowering urge left me with no option but to visit the nearest beer garden as soon as I arrived in St Mary's township in Chitungwiza. I wished to celebrate sweet homecoming. And the chance meeting, with a little of the alcohol that had separated us.

"You can have that for beer, or rather alcohol." The words rang again and again in my head as I enjoyed my beer later that night in Machembere Beer Garden.

BABABULELE

John S. Read

Dry dust drips off the Shu-Shine bus,
brakes squealing with the rural road residues.
Jacketed and blanketed bodies boiling out,
voices chatter, rise and fall.
Silence settles in an interval of inactivity.
Bus crew carry bags out of the winter night;
Child cries into his mother's arms.

Frail, a final form shields eyes under bar lights
released into the empty street,
a neat wind creases his eyes
closed, but a cracked mouth opens
in an old man's mute appeal.
Stripped as his history, the lips'
lost syllables slip into the empty street
drying in a lost night where his story lies.
*"Indodana labatwana bayo bababulele."**

"My son and his children, they have killed them."

17

THE CHICKEN BUS

Linda Msebele

I stand with my back arched and my behind sticking out, I hold fast to the metal rod above my head. Harshly, he tells me to face the window and, grabbing me around the waist, he pushes me around. After an emotional and draining day at work, I am too tired to tell him off. Besides, I have no choice but to comply, he is the man in charge and, if I give him trouble, he will simply throw me off. Out to the desperate pickpockets, waiting in the night.

I am on a chicken bus. A chicken bus is an ugly bus, nothing like the sleek and fancy buses from overseas. It was designed especially for our rural dust roads, roads that collapse into ditches and mini dams during the rainy season. It is the cheapest, and certainly the harshest, way of getting home these days. Such travelling is meant for those like me (believe me, there are millions like me) who cannot afford the emergency taxis that ply the same route and that charge a much higher fee.

It is noisy, stuffy and smelly in here. The shortage of water in the city does not help; the water rationing means we often go days without water. It's hardly surprising that so many find it easy to give up washing, it takes so much effort to get water. It really stinks in here. It stinks of poverty. It's nothing like the chic smell of the wealthy. I try to slide the tiny window-pane open to allow in some air, but to no avail. The thing will not budge. I'm not surprised. Many of these buses had long been forgotten, brought back to uneasy life from the scrap-yard by bus companies keen to cash in on the transport crisis. These buses can only operate at the cheap price they do by cutting down on maintenance and comfort.

Someone pushing and shoving jostles me out of my thoughts. The bloody person is almost bending me out of shape. I feel annoyance rising within me. Turning, I come face to face with an elderly woman carrying a 10kg bag of sugar on her head. She has nowhere to put it down and no one seated is willing to hold it for her; they look away, pretend not to see, pretend that they have forgotten that it is traditional to assist your elders. She gives me a warm but tired smile, and I smile back and hope to God that my smile will take away some of her tiredness. I feel tired even as I smile, I feel beaten and disfigured by poverty, by a fading hope that some day soon, all will be fine, just fine.

My eyes shift from her smiling face to stare at the valuable commodity on her head. There is a severe shortage of sugar and I am shocked, and not a little envious, to see the bag on the old woman's head.

"Where did you buy the sugar, Gogo?" It is hard not to ask. I swallow with longing as I wait for her to answer.

"I got it from a supermarket down town, but it is long finished. I was one of the lucky ones to get it after I queued for the whole day in a dirty alley."

Nowadays supermarket managers make people queue in narrow, filthy alleys so that they can be easily controlled by riot police. People kill for sugar these days. I read it in the paper, in the *Chronicle*. A mob tore down the wall of a supermarket in Entumbane, killing a security guard who was trying to bring order to the queue. Sugar is serious business. The old woman is excited when she tells me that she survived beatings from the riot police who tried to control the angry, hungry crowd. She is like a triumphant hero returning from war.

There is virtually nothing on the supermarket shelves these days. People went crazy in those heady days of the price slashes, when it seemed as if even they, the strugglers, the long sufferers, the punch bags of inflation, could finally afford some food, some clothing, some of the decencies of life. Those people who ran around the shops, grabbing this and grabbing that, with crazily jubilant smiles, are still running around today. They are no longer smiling, believe me, they have fixed, desperate, pleading looks as they scour the shops for anything to buy. The winding queues are filled with the long suffering and the morose.

I look at myself, I look at those in the bus with me, the chicken bus clients. Their skins tell stories of tough lives, of desperation, of living on the edge. I know that they, like me, are eating boiled vegetables every day. I know that they too fret about the power cuts and the water cuts. I know that they too cannot afford to have boreholes drilled on their properties, cannot afford to buy inverters like the well-to-do in the low density areas. We are the chicken

19

bus clients, we are the desperate poor of Zimbabwe.

How different the realities of life can be. Some people drive the latest *Mercedes*, *BMWs* and *Pajeros*. I wonder how they manage to make money in a country with such an inflationary and depressed economy. What do they know that I do not? Am I doomed to forever board chicken buses? How the hell do some people make money while so many of us are eating water for dinner and having salt for dessert? Some of these people thank God for the situation in the country. Surely, they are mad, how can one thank God for riches that are built upon the tears and bitterness of so many, so many whose bellies are buddies with rumbles of hunger? How can their eyes be blind to the grim, the defeated, the pained and the bemused faces of their fellow Zimbabweans? How can they shut out the talk about never ending queues – borehole queues, bus queues, bread queues, mealie-meal queues, sugar queues, fuel queues? All these shortages, all these needs not met. Will we, the chicken bus clients, ever know the joys of a good life again?

I am grateful to be standing next to a woman in this crowded bus. It would be a misfortune to stand in front of a man with hot blood and a keen erection. Believe me, many have stood behind me in the past. Such men press close, sway with every move the bus makes, yet, miraculously, remain stuck fast to your butt, their erections hot and uncomfortable, unrelenting and hungry. I dislike such men. I dislike unwelcome erections on my butt. I wish to yank them by their penises and throw them out of the chicken bus. The penises of these men have to salute every female butt they encounter. Bloody men. Bloody chicken buses. Bloody poverty. Bloody Zimbabwe.

Someone is pushing me. I instinctively stand aside because I know that some people will be getting off at the next stop. It's always wise to be quick to move. Some rough character could easily shout at me to ventilate their frustration. It's not only rough characters these days; there is just too much suffering now, people are edgy, the slightest thing sets them off. I like to imagine that we are nuts in a frying pan with the heat on, some of us pop our nut skins faster than others. Some of us turn black faster than others, the bottom line is that we are all being roasted.

"My sie, you are standing on my toes."

I move aside with alacrity, concerned, afraid that I could set off some bitter mouthing.

"Don't worry my sie, it's crowded in here."

He is smiling easily at me. He is not really bothered at all that I am stepping on his feet. He is one of the few good ones, the ones who won't let poverty beat them, the ones who refuse to turn sour, the ones who won't let fear cloud their brows, the ones who still smile. It's such a relief to meet one, so rare these days. I smile back at him. He winks at me. I wink back. We both burst out laughing, we are pleased by our lightness, our humanness. The bitter complaining sounds distant to me now that I am warmed by laughing and smiling at someone who still remembers that it is possible to smile, to laugh and to wink.

When I eventually escape from the chicken bus at my stop, my feelings of warmth have not grown cold. At this moment, at least, remembering the shared laughter, I feel hope rising in me.

THE CRACKED, PINK LIPS OF ROSIE'S BRIDEGROOM

Petina Gappah

The wedding guests look upon the cracked, pink lips of Rosie's bridegroom. They look at Rosie's own lips that owe their reddish pinkness to artifice, they think, and not disease. Can Rosie see what they see, they wonder, that her newly made husband's sickness screams out its presence from every pore? Disease flourishes in the slipperiness of his tufted hair; it is alive in the darkening skin, in the whites of the eyes whiter than nature intended, in the violently pink-red lips, the blood beneath fighting to erupt through the broken skin.

He smiles often, Rosie's bridegroom. He smiles when a drunken aunt entertains the guests with a dance that, outside this celebration of sanctioned fornication, could be called obscene. He smiles when an uncle based in Manchester, England, calls the cell-phone of his son and sends his congratulations across nine thousand kilometres shortened by *Vodafone* on his end and *Econet* on the other. His smile broadens as the son tells the master of ceremonies that the uncle pledges two hundred pounds as a wedding gift, the smile becomes broader still when the master of ceremonies announces that the gift is worth two hundred billion dollars on Zimbabwe's parallel market. He smiles and smiles and smiles and his smile reveals the heightened colour of his gums.

They sit in the rented marquee from Rooney's, the wedding guests. The marquee is resplendent in the wedding colours chosen by Rosie, cream and buttermilk, with gold to provide the contrast. They chew rice and chicken on the bone and wash it down with mouthfuls of bottled fizzy drinks, beer and an intensive colloquy on Rosie's bridegroom's reputation. This is his second marriage, everyone knows. He buried one wife already, even Rosie knows. What Rosie doesn't know: he also buried two girlfriends, possibly more. The evidentiary weight of his appearance, circumstantial in isolation, is corroborated not only by the death of one wife and two girlfriends, but by other incidents in the life of Rosie's bridegroom.

For instance: it is known that he was often in the company of Memory, now late, formerly of Glen View Three, notorious Memory with men from here to Kuwadzana, Memory who died with her cracked lips (also pinkened) protesting at her leaving.

Another thing: he drank nightly at the illegal shebeen at MaiTatenda's house, with MaiTatenda who has one Tatenda and no BabaTatenda, MaiTatenda who provided her clients with home comforts and then some, MaiTatenda who was seen only last week, just skin and bones, coughing – coughing and shivering in this sweltering December. One doesn't want to be unkind of course, they say, but that is what happens to whores who wrap their legs around men that are not their husbands.

And finally, incontrovertibly: Rosie's bridegroom's car was seen parked outside the house of a prophet who lives in Muhacha Crescent in Warren Park, he of the hands that can drive out the devil Satan who has chosen to appear as an incurable virus in their midst. This prophet has placed an advert in all the newspapers. He responded to that advert, Rosie's new husband, he must have, for his car, the silver *Toyota Camry* that was always in front of MaiTatenda's house, was seen outside of the house of the prophet.

Is any Sick among You? the advert says, *Let him call for the Elders of the Church; and let them Pray over him, Anointing him with Oil in the Name of the Lord. And the Prayer of Faith shall save the sick, JAMES 5:13-15. Jesus of Nazareth Saves*, the advert says. *Come to have His healing Hands placed upon your Troubled Hearts. All Illnesses Cured. For Nothing shall be Impossible with the Lord, GENESIS 18:14.*

There is but one disease that drives men to turn their *Toyota Camrys*, their *Mercedes Benzes, Pajeros, BMWs* in the direction of Warren Park. There is only one illness that pushes both the well-wheeled and un-wheeled to seek out the prophet. It is the big disease with the little name, the sickness that no one dies of, the disease whose real name is unspoken, the sickness that speaks its presence through the pink redness of lips, the slipperiness of hair, through the whites of the eyes whiter than nature intended.

23

They are gifted with prophecy, the wedding guests, they look at Rosie's bridegroom's lips and in them see Rosie's fate. She will die first, of course, for that is the pattern, the woman first, and then the man. The woman first, leaving the man to marry again, to marry another woman who will also die first. They will keen loudly at Rosie's wake; they will fall into each other's arms. Their first tears shed, they will talk of the manner of her death.

In the public spaces they will say: She just fell sick. Just like that, no warning, nothing. She woke up in the morning; she prepared food for the family. Around eleven she said: My head, my head. And by the time she should have cooked the supper, she was gone. So quickly, they will say. No one can comprehend the speed with which it happened. It burdens the heart, they will say. Where have you heard that a person dies from a headache?

But in the dark corners away from the public spaces they will say: *Haiwa*, we knew all along. Her death was there in the bright pink lips of her bridegroom, how far did she think it could go? Remember the first wife, remember Memory, remember MaiTatenda, remember the two girlfriends, possibly more?

How far did she think it would go?

And they sit now, the wedding guests, passing rice and chicken through their own reddened lips, complaining that there is not enough to eat, not enough to drink, they sit watching, calculating, wondering, how many of them will be there to see that death.

ECHOES OF SILENCE

Raisedon Baya

The heat bounced off the rocky earth and floated aimlessly around the village. It was intense. Walking in the open was torture. The heat scalded the skin with its hot, invisible tongue. It sucked at glands and veins in a determined attempt to incapacitate. The sun and Mother Earth seemed to be conspiring together to incinerate all living things.

High up, the blue, corrupt sky promised nothing. The rivers were dry. The soil, taking a cue from the sun, was busy swallowing life and everything else upon which it could lay its hands. The few crops and plants that had miraculously managed to push their way out of the soil found it impossible to survive, let alone smile. Once out the plants found themselves fighting a war on two fronts. From below the soil tried to strangle them from the roots and from above the ruthless sun roasted them.

The drought had reduced everyone to a beggar. People were going back to eating roots and experimenting with drought resistant plants. Animals were dropping dead from the heat and hunger. Those that were still soldiering on looked emaciated and as if they were all suffering from a terrible disease that was eating them from inside. Death stared at every movement they made with hungry and excited eyes.

Khayelihle came out of the hut where she had been trying to cook dried vegetables for the evening meal. She had burnt most of them anyway. The vegetables had come from a relative who lived some villages away, on the other side of the mountain. Her brother had had to walk for a whole day, crossing the mountain and the dry river, to the other village for the vegetables. They were a mixture of rape, tsunga, tshomolia and cabbage that had been

25

boiled together, sprinkled with salt, and then left in the sun to dry. When she walked out of the hut, with smoke pinching her eyes, Khayelihle smelled of nothing but the burnt vegetables and the smoke. She wiped her eyes and looked for her goatskin mat that was behind her brother's hut.

Khayelihle was young, dark and almost beautiful. She beat the mat against the big baobab tree and released a cloud of dust that rose excitedly towards the sky, before realising the sky was too far away and drifted back to settle. The big baobab tree that offered some shade stood sandwiched by two huts. She threw the mat on the ground and lowered herself to rest.

She was hot and tired. She wanted a bath. The heat was too much. She longed for the cold, slippery hug of the river water. She missed the feel of the water cascading down her body in small rivers. Before the drought, the river had run, circling the village and then disappearing into the woodlands. Bathing in the river used to free her spirit. There was something about running water, its cold touch, its freshness and the promise it made to her skin, that tickled and made her laugh with abandon. This and the act of being completely naked in the open drugged her and left her feeling high and good about herself. Bathing in the river had always brought her closer to herself, closer to nature.

But all that was gone. There was no water in the river; it was now as dry as the fire place in the morning. The sand and stones that used to be hidden by the water now stood bare, unprotected from the sun.

In the sand of the river-bed, villagers had started digging wells in a vain attempt to follow the water to where it had retreated away from the reach of the sun's invisible tongue. There was only one place with water, near the mountain. Here the water was dark, still and stale. It was here that animals, from the mountain and around the village, came to drink. Men from the village could be found bathing at this pool. This was all before the coming of the soldiers.

Fear had descended on the village, riding in an army truck and wearing a soldier's uniform, wrapping itself around people's necks to make breathing a difficult task. It banished laughter from the village. It chained people to their homesteads. It fenced compounds, barricaded paths and roads and permeated even into the privacy of bedrooms. The soldiers had come from the city, speaking a strange language.

Two days after arriving at the village they came across an old man bathing at the pool with his son and took them prisoners. They ordered the son to masturbate his father before taking both to the business centre. There they paraded them naked for the better part of the day and, when darkness came, one of them opened fire. Father and son were dead. Shot in cold blood. This incident sent shock waves to all corners of the village. Men in the village became afraid to make love to their wives lest the soldiers burst into the bedrooms and order them to continue making love while they watched or even took them to the business centre to amuse other soldiers. So bedrooms became more like hiding places than places of affection and love.

Khayelihle was twenty-two years old. She had just reached that point in her life where she was waiting for the right man to come and ask for her hand in marriage. She had great treasures in her hands, in her voice and in her womb. Treasures she wanted to offer to the man who would come knocking at her door, wanting to share his life with her. Treasures she had clung to and guarded so jealously. She had no boyfriend. Boyfriends were a waste of time. She wanted a man to marry, someone with whom she could have babies. She wanted her own home, her own fields and to be called by her own children's names.

The goatskin mat she was sleeping on was hard and uncomfortable. But she was used to it. She lay under the shade of the big baobab tree and tried to dream about this man she was waiting for, this man who would come asking for her hand. She dozed off, still trying to put a face to this man, still trying to decide how many children she would have, and what their names would be.

Sihle. Ntombi. Butho. Bafana. Four children would do. She didn't want too many. That was how the soldiers found her. Curled up in a ball and dreaming about children. Her own children.

Khayelihle woke up into a nightmare. She was dying, in the very process of losing herself. She was dying from the inside. She felt her insides shrivel as the intruder destroyed her innocent hopes, hitting at the very bones of her womanhood, breaking her into bits and pieces of death.

She died that day, that afternoon. She died under the big baobab tree while the gigantic mountain that, all her life, had promised her protection stood and looked the other way. She died trying to scream and the mountain refused to listen. She died alone, died a terrible, violent death that left no smell or trail. It was a death that started between her legs and, cancer-like, spread to every part of her body. Lying on the goatskin mat she felt the excitement about family and motherhood wilting and dying like the crops in the fields. She felt her insides burning, the wetness between her legs scalding her thighs and slowly erasing all her dreams.

Then she heard her brother running towards her. He must have seen her

27

dying and was coming to rescue her. He was almost at the gate, screaming her name, when other soldiers materialized from behind the huts and cut his run short. With guns raised towards him, the soldiers fired questions, poked at his stomach and chest with their guns. Khayelihle wanted to stand up, she wanted to run to the soldiers and plead for him. She wanted to beg for mercy, but she had no energy to stand up and beg, the wetness tied her hands and legs and imprisoned her and so she lay there, in pain, and watched as the soldiers, looking like a pack of scavengers, dragged her brother towards the mountain.

That was the last time she saw her brother. Nothing was ever seen or heard of him. Her dreams became ashes. She never dreamt about a suitor or children or happiness again.

Long after the soldiers had gone back to wherever they had come from, fear hung over the whole village like heavy grey clouds threatening to unleash a flood reminiscent of Noah's time. It was a solid, choking silence that descended on the people and wrapped itself around their throats. The silence was everywhere. It was in the dust that greeted them the minute they stepped off the chicken buses from the city and set foot in the village, in the food they ate, the water they drank and on the beds they slept in at night. But it was in the eyes and the heaviness of their voices that this fear was most manifest.

This fear, this silence, consumed them as they walked, it was with them as they slept and tried to dream again. It gnawed at their inner beings, nibbled softly and slowly at their spirits and then left them for dead. The living dead of this country. Walking village corpses that secretly awaited resurrection. People in the village walked in silence, they ate in silence. Even their love-making became a silent ritual.

This silence became a way of life, deeply entrenched in their system. It became their death. Secretly, in the comfort of their bedrooms, they all longed for freedom. Freedom from this corrosive and suffocating silence, from the heaviness of their tongues. They all wished for the day when they would wake up with the courage to lift their tongues and wag them defiantly like aggressive Alsatian dogs wagging their tails. They prayed for that day. The day of freedom.

Not everyone believed in the power of prayer. There were those that stood up and tried shaking this silence off their tongues. A few, straight from higher institutions of learning and armed to the teeth with words and sentences nicely strung together, tried to incite the people against silence. They told the people that tongues were meant to move, to dance, to throw words out of the caves they called mouths. They warned that words kept for too long in the mouth would become stale and end up choking them.

These young activists against silence were immediately branded as dangerous. Terrorists. Sellouts. Some were quickly bribed back into silence. One or two stubborn ones were picked up in the dead of night and dressed in heavier, more frightening, silence. When they came back to the village they couldn't even whisper their own names to their own mothers. They hid in their homes and confronted their nightmares with heavy tongues that refused to let them scream for help.

Whatever it was the soldiers left behind, whatever they did, no one in the village wanted to talk about it. Those that tried, only whispered it in dark places and only to people they trusted.

By the time the soldiers left the village Khayelihle realised that something was growing inside her. Khayelihle died once more. But like a cat she discovered she had more than one life. Deeply disturbed, she kept to herself and watched the sun rise from the other side of the mountain and set with the promise of nothing better tomorrow. With each rising and setting, her stomach grew.

Finally it was time for the child to come. That day it rained. Heavy rain. While Khayelihle cried and pushed in pain and the midwife tried to make the process fast and less painful, it thundered, roared and poured. Lightning welcomed the child. Khayelihle's cries and the child's silent entry into the world were swallowed by the roaring rain. As the child came out of the womb, mouth wide open in an effort to cry, the midwife heard nothing. The child's tongue was too heavy for him to cry. It was a tongue burdened with secrets, secrets only shared by his mother. His hands were rolled up into tiny fists as if holding tightly to the secrets.

The big baobab tree and the mountain, both drenched in shame and rain, looked at each other with conspiratorial glances. They both wanted to question the silence of the child. But how could they ask when both had been there when Khayelihle had died her first death, when both had failed to protect her? What right did they have now to ask her about the silence of her child? And so the big baobab tree and the mountain held their tongues and remained silent.

Khayelihle embraced her child and wrapped him in the comfort of her smiles and warm hands. Just as she had accepted her first death she also accepted this silent child. She tried to love him, to separate him from her own

29

death, from the nightmares that constantly assaulted her at night. The child gave her a new reason to want to see the next day, hope for a rebirth. Her own resurrection. The child looked innocent. He was. A child is a gift from God and the ancestors.

She called him Fanyana. Small boy.

No one celebrated the birth of Fanyana. People whispered about the silent child. They wondered who had sired him. They wanted to know this man, to put a face to him. But Khayelihle kept the face of this man to herself. She did not know his name. She did not want to know it. So when people stopped her around the village wanting to know who Fanyana's father was, she simply told them: "Fanyana has no father."

The identity of Fanyana's father was hidden under Fanyana's tongue. A tongue that does not dance.

HWANGE

Andrew Pocock

Acacia, teak and false mopane,
Leadwood, white thorn, plain and pan
Bake beneath the skies of Hwange,
Where rhino matter more than man.

Bush exists for bush alone –
Let's not seek another reason;
Fathers forth the sable, roan,
Impala, kudu in their season.

Drive the endless, whitening road
Unwinding into mystery.
Feather, scale and mud on hide:
Textures of prehistory.

Don't be fooled. This timelessness
Is fragile as a morning's mist.
What yesterday has put in place
Tomorrow holds, in palm or fist.

FICTION

Brian Chikwava

After staring ponderingly into the middle distance, she sighed. "Anyway," she said, striking a peculiarly weary pose and lowering her head to continue knitting. She was unimpressed this time. My lightning conductor, that's what she had always been, and I had always been her favourite nephew. Now the woman sat old and immovable on the floor of her verandah.

My father and his snake skin belt – a partnership whose thrashingly blinding efficacy was beyond doubt. Going home without Auntie MaNdlo? Laughable stupidity that. She was the only creature mother and father always deferred to. They would never touch me if she pleaded my case.

"Brian Chikwava," she read my name out loud. It was printed on my trunk.

"Brian Chikwava." A derisive tone. She was not saying it to me but merely enjoying the way my name rolled off her tongue. My trunk shone extraordinarily black and heavy, ominous on the verandah floor where I had dumped it on arrival.

"Chikwava's son." This time she laughed and shook her head.

On this occasion, the usual sympathy stimulating excuses – a dining hall that always smelled of burnt *sadza* and soggy cabbage, wiry mattresses, janitors who never bothered with the boiler so that hot water ran out after only half the hostel residents had showered and howling mad hostel masters – had failed. The senior boys called us names. They call me names Auntie MaNdlo, I said to myself. Sounded pathetic; she would fall off the edge of the verandah laughing if I said it out loud.

"I think…," I said hesitatingly after an uncomfortable silence. Auntie MaNdlo knitted and hummed. She liked honest people.

"I think I was wrong to run away from school." I had to come clean to have any hope of winning her over; that way there was, at least, a chance that she would sympathise, accompany me home and I would be taken back to school the following day, face my due punishment and soon all would be forgotten. A whole week's afternoons with the caretaker, Mr Mpofu, and I would have paid for my misdemeanours. Mr Mpofu could up the work rate of almost any stubborn chain gang in any prison anywhere on the planet. Still that seemed the best option now. With this woman being this oddly frosty, any chances of being moved to a different school had all but vanished.

"I don't know what got into me," I said, wringing my wrist. Auntie MaNdlo continued humming. Not looking at me.

"It's a good school really. We have good teachers." I tried to think of appropriately positive things to say; tell her about our good teachers. Sagging on the sisal armchair that she had fetched for me on arrival, I felt my armpits moisten. Beyond the verandah roof the sun snarled, fierce and, on surrounding mopane trees, cicadas shrieked. My tie was tight around my neck, my blazer heavy on my shoulders. "We have good teachers," I said unconvincingly, struggling to find a starting point.

The first teacher to reveal his face inside my head was Mr Chiwange; if you were a school head with a badly disciplined metalwork class and were in need of a no-frills, fearsome old grumpy disciplinarian who'd get to the try square before any of the class and throw it, without irony, in the direction of the disruptive thing, then he was a sensible option to employ. But he had called me 'vacant'. I couldn't possibly say nice things about him.

"Mr Gono…" He was our mathematics teacher; a big bear of a man. Kg for dollar, he was the best value any school head could get.

"He has a good sense of humour. Sometimes he picks mathematical equations from the textbook and demonstrates on the board how to go about solving them. If you ask him why his answer is 47 while the textbook says it should be 49, he simply says 'just add two.' He's a good laugh. And a good teacher."

Auntie MaNdlo swatted a fly with an old newspaper and continued knitting.

"Mr Gono used to be friends with Baboon." I was beginning to hit my stride now. Baboon was our English teacher, so called because of a penchant for the word 'baboon' – '...and if you have spelling corrections to make, you write the word that you misspelt three times across the page; if the word is 'baboon', you write 'baboon baboon baboon',' he loved to say. Once he repeatedly slapped Robert on the face because he thought he was laughing during the lesson: 'He's still smiling,' Baboon said, walking back from the front of the classroom for the fourth time in a minute. Slap slap. 'I will make him cry in the end, just you watch.' Robert's buck-teeth by then stuck out of a determined and bravely fixed grin of soundless anguish, eyes glazed with tears. 'Look, he's still smiling this boy. Do you see his teeth? What is that, you tell me?' Slap slap.

Baboon would leave the school in my final year. That's after his wife threw hot cooking oil at his face in the heat of a row.

"Rati!" Auntie MaNdlo shouted.

"Ma!" Rati, her ten year old daughter, answered.

"Bring me a glass of cold water."

I cleared my throat to get Auntie MaNdlo's attention. She started humming again. Indifferently.

"We also have Mr Gushungo. He is our housemaster but he is also a history teacher. He is a classic teacher who brings lots of enthusiasm, stimulation and trickery into the classroom and dormitory corridors. My friend, Khulani, once shot out of our classroom and ran straight into Mr Gushungo, who was on his way to another classroom carrying a high pile of exercise books. Khulani had to pick them off the floor one by one while Mr. Gushungo stood by tall and silent. When he was presented with the neat pile, Mr. Gushungo said that Khulani was a remarkably energetic young man who was clearly a keen athlete to be running in school corridors like that. 'I am curious to find out how long it will take you to run six laps on the athletics track,' he said. It was an October afternoon, 37 degrees Celsius, and the track lay shimmering and melting in the middle of the school estate. When he satisfied Mr. Gushungo's curiosity, Khulani was panting impressively like a dog and his tongue hung out to his knees.

"He is the only teacher who, like the senior boys, calls us blue stomachs because we are first years. 'Ey, blue stomachs, is it so hard to make your beds properly?' he always says when he inspects us in our dormitory before we go to the hall for assembly. I love it."

"What does blue stomach mean?" Auntie MaNdlo was thawing, though still not making eye contact.

"Ah, it's a kind of lizard; you find them on lots of big trees at our school. It has a blue stomach. We first years are called blue stomachs because our jerseys are blue instead of grey, which is what senior boys wear. But that's okay because they say at the end of the year you lose your tail, your stomach ceases to be blue and you became a human being again when you come back for your second year."

"Rati!"

"Ma!"

"Do I have to wait for the rains before I can get a glass of water?"

Auntie MaNdlo started humming a song again.

"Anyway, Mr Gushungo is a nice man. Even if he had a punch up with Baboon one night when Baboon got drunk at his house and started singing in a disorderly manner in the middle of the night. They live in the teachers' houses behind our hostel."

Rati emerged from the door carrying a glass of water. She hurriedly put it down on the cement screed floor and was turning to dash away when Auntie MaNdlo lassoed her back. "You, Moyo's daughter. What has got into you? What kind of manners are those? Are you running to catch the last train to the moon or what?"

Rati, now having spun round, stood silent, legs crossed, hands clasped behind her back in total submission.

"Bring me ice."

"We also have a good library, really. And the librarian, Mr. Mudede, he's a nice man too. And keeps the library in order; every shelf is nicely labelled and occasionally he helps you find books. 'What is the difference between literature and fiction,' one of my classmates asked him last month. 'Literature is what was written by people that are now dead, and fiction is by people that continue to live,' he told us. Good man that one. He nearly throttled a fourth year who held a different and embarrassingly ignorant opinion. But this is fiction Auntie MaNdlo," I startled myself with a laugh.

This time Auntie MaNdlo stopped knitting, turned her head and stared at me. I smiled, gave her imploring, soppy eyes.

It is fiction. This.

THE FIRST LADY'S YELLOW SHOES

Peter Ncube

The President felt the presence of his wife in the room. He sat still in his chair, his face a few centimetres from the French window while her perfume swirled around his head.

"We have to leave now, father of Tendai," she said in a small voice.

"Have you finished the packing?"

"Our suitcases are packed, sir."

The President swayed to his feet. A dull ache in his head made him wince. He moved closer to the windowpane and tilted his head forward until his glasses clinked against the cold glass.

"Are the children fine?"

"The girl is very calm about it, sir. But Tendai is close to weeping."

"He is a silly boy. He's telling himself – no more play station, no burgers and chips. Go calm the child and tell him this is the beginning of his new life as a man. He's now a commoner like everyone else. Let's see what he makes of himself. As for my daughter, who can touch my brave daughter? Aaah… I need a few more minutes of this view of our lovely garden. Only thing I'll miss about this house, this view of the garden at this time of the evening. It's the colours, I think. The pink of those roses, the green of the lawn. To think – twenty years of my life I was locked up in a room with no view, and tomorrow I might wake up in another room with no view."

The First Lady was silent for a moment. Her view to the world was a different one.

"Ah, sir..." her voice was tentative.

"What else is there, mother of Tendai?"

"My yellow shoes, sir. I can't find them."

The President turned around to face her, a frown on his face. He thought she had at least a hundred pairs of shoes.

"What are you talking about?"

"My yellow shoes, sir. I can't find them. The Hong Kong ones."

The President was still for a moment. Then he straightened his long thin frame and smiled at her.

"I can't believe you're talking about shoes at a moment like this. Yellow shoes? Are you sure you had shoes of that colour? I've never seen any yellow shoes in this house."

"The ones you bought for me in Hong Kong, sir. In a little Chinese shop..."

The old man turned his back to her and breathed onto the windowpane. She was in a state of shock: that could be the only explanation. Yellow shoes in a Chinese shop in Hong Kong? All the shops in Hong Kong were Chinese, were they not? Besides, when last had they been to that city? Before or after the Chinese takeover? Ten, fifteen, twenty years ago? He couldn't quite remember. There was nothing remarkable about Hong Kong, or Hanoi, or Beijing, or Karachi, or Caracas... All those places were nothing but a blur through which his motorcade zipped; they were strange flags swaying to the beat of strange national anthems and the guards of honour and the butterfly dances at the airports when they welcomed him; they were the choking fragrances of expensive hotel rooms. The hotel rooms he could do without, but the butterfly dances at the airports, the adulation... Now they would never again receive him that way at airports. No longer would there be clanging drums and songs and smiling kids with bouquets in hand. All because some American idiot had decided to label him a dictator, which of course he wasn't. Neither had he ever been the angel they had thought he was. First they brand you an angel and stick wings on you and you find yourself flying and when you protest that this is not me, they pluck the wings off and suddenly you become not just a plucked angel falling down fast, but the Devil himself. A dictator, a pariah, a maniac; a man-eating savage waiting to be toppled and paraded before the CNN cameras, lurking from behind the bars of a Hague prison.

So, to confound one American idiot and his band of cheerleaders, he had held the cleanest African election ever. No doctored voters' roll, no dead men voting. No beating up of voters, no army or police intervention in peaceful rallies. And, most importantly, every man and every woman in the land who had an ID, passport or driver's licence could vote at any polling station in the land.

"We'll show our detractors what democracy means, these same governments that just yesterday were labelling us as terrorists, fit only to be second-class citizens in this, the land of our forefathers, the land of our spirits, our totems, our umbilical cords…"

But this bluff-gimmick had backfired in horrible fashion. The people had listened to the American idiot and overwhelmingly voted for the opposition, and here he was, vacating State House and the soon-to-be former First Lady was ranting on about yellow shoes, and Chinese shops, and Hong Kong.

He just wasn't interested in her yellow shoes. He had bigger worries. The blunt eviction notice he had been served with: twenty-four hours, or else. The tenant-in-waiting, an uncouth former factory worker, couldn't wait to move in. The povo couldn't wait. They had cast their votes and had decided he had to vacate this palace, this theatre of the African Dream, this Valhalla. The People Had Spoken. And all his dear wife could think of was yellow shoes bought in a Chinese shop in Hong Kong many, many years ago.

"Stop talking nonsense, woman. Just go tell Bigboy to check that helicopter for me while you bring the children. We'll leave as soon as it gets dark."

He turned away from her and sat in the rocking chair next to the big French window. Beyond the garden was an electrified fence, and further on the sun was menstruating down the twin glass facades of the Independence Hotel. He shifted his gaze back to the beautiful garden, the pink roses amid the tiny yellow flowers he had brought from… was it Hiroshima, or Hawaii? Or Hanoi, or Hong Kong? He couldn't remember.

He didn't hear the door open behind him but the discreet cough made him turn around. The massive man in black T-shirt, black jeans, and black takkies had a voice deep and rumbling and hoarse, a dark voice that jangled the nerves.

"Sir, we have a minor problem."

"What is it, Bigboy?"

"Mother of Tendai is being… difficult, sir."

"What do you mean?"

"She says she won't come without her yellow shoes. The children are trying to calm her and she's screaming at them to find her yellow shoes."

"Go bring her, Bigboy. Go bring them all. Use whatever force is necessary for her to understand our situation."

Bigboy turned and disappeared in silence. The soles of his shoes were, as always, of the padded kind, as silent as the blackness around him.

In a few minutes he was back, behind a red-eyed First Lady, her teenage son, and a daughter who seemed little affected by what was going on. This was his family, these three souls and the big bodyguard he had plucked from the gallows two decades ago. The Mutilator. The man had committed a crime of passion so brutal the papers had executed him even before the President had appended his signature to the death warrant. When the execution came it was done with so much secrecy and magic that a Bigboy had arisen from the ashes of The Mutilator.

"You all know the outcome of the elections. We are no longer the First Family. Meaning we are no longer the tenants of this house. We have to go. Don't ask me where we're going – we just have to get out of here fast. Our many friends throughout the world will take care of us. We have money; we have homes, some of which you have already stayed in. We'll go to one of them now. Bigboy, lead the way."

They followed the big bodyguard in single file, daughter, son, mother, father, hurrying down the silent corridors of what had been home for the children's entire lives, and for half that of the First Lady. She was an accessory that the President had looked for to make his old age comfortable and now she was weeping and swaying in front of him, unwilling to be torn away from her yellow shoes. She had come only a decade and a half ago, pregnant with his son, and the little girl that had followed many years later had the mother's short bones and the father's small hard eyes and sharp brains and sense of purpose. If only she had grown fast, she would have been the next President.

They emerged into the dawn to be met by the sight of a helicopter in flames. Bigboy quickly pushed everyone back into the house. He was a big solid man who could think on his feet and now he was half-running down the corridors again and opening the door to a room that had nothing but a black wall-to-wall carpet and a single light bulb burning from the ceiling. He carefully locked the door when everyone was in the room. After that he went to a corner, rolled back the carpet and stamped hard on the wooden floor. On the third such stamp, the whole floor began to descend and the President fought to contain the bile bubbling up his throat. Twenty seconds of slow descent later, when he was just getting used to the idea of this room-elevator, the lift creaked to a stop, and there was a yellow door that led into a well-lit tunnel that looked like an underground station. But instead of a train, there was a small grey car, a *Nissan Sunny* of the late nineties. Bigboy held out the keys to the President.

"The tank is full. Drive straight down the tunnel and you'll come out into a side street that leads straight into Anwar Sadat Avenue. Drive straight down towards Greenland Township, don't turn left or right. Drive slowly into the township, there's not much going on down there but you don't want to be attracting attention. After the first school on your left, there'll be a stadium. Turn right immediately after the stadium and look for the sixth house on your left – that's your home for today. There's a couple living there, they'll be expecting you. They'll give you food and show you where to sleep for the night. Wait for me there until I have made a plan to get you to safety. Don't attempt to leave the city, don't communicate with anyone. I will see you later, Mr President."

He turned and shut the door behind him and there was a slight vibration as Bigboy raised himself back to the house.

The President opened the door and sank into the driver's seat, his wife beside him, and the two children on the back seat. Many decades had passed since he'd driven a car, but this model held no secrets for him. It started at a single turn of the key and he guided it round a small bend to the left and another to the right and the tunnel slid deeper into the earth and then after a short steep rise he emerged into the cold night and sirens and car horns screamed everywhere and the horizon was ablaze with fireworks. The capital was celebrating, the whole country was ululating, but he hadn't been invited. He wondered if he would ever again be invited to any birthday, any funeral, any opening of a school or clinic or road.

"Stop!" the First Lady commanded. He slowed down and parked by the side of the road. Before the car could fully come to a stop, his wife yanked the door open, jumped out and dashed into a shop, her handbag flailing like a sledgehammer. It was a shoe shop. The yellow shoes. Without thinking, he put the car into gear and sped off towards the safe house in Greenland Township. He had no time for theatrics. He had to save his skin, and the skins of his son and, most of all, this daughter who was now rolling in laughter on the back seat while her brother screamed for him to stop. But he did not stop. Instead, he increased speed and soon began laughing too, and, as the sun rose above the grey township of Greenland, he realized that his forty two years in power, his attempt to shape the minds and lives of a nation and a continent by word and by sword – all that was an anecdote. What mattered most was the laughter he shared at this moment with his beloved daughter who would have, if given a chance, made such a wonderful leader.

FIRST RAIN

Judy Maposa

It is a dream.

A grown woman's naked form glides into the clearing. Her steps are proud and firm, yet silent. In the open she stops, lifts her arms high above her head and starts swaying at the waist.

Her body is ripe, proud and all woman. Head tilted back and eyes piercing the depths of the moonlit sky she continues the slow sway. Her feet start to move in delicate steps, forwards, backwards in a shuffle dance. Every now and then she bends slightly at the waist, accentuating the curve of a generous bum.

A murmur rises from unseen spectators, which turns into a primitive chant. She dances, intent and silent. I am she, yet I watch her. I feel her quickening heartbeat. I feel her desire for a release. I am one with her in begging the sky.

Her face glistens with the sweat of her effort and yet she continues the dance. She will not stop until the release comes. Rivulets slither down her forehead, her neck, her breasts and down the small of her back.

Now I hear the drums whose beat rises and falls in time with the chanting. The drums pick up a new plaintive beat, so loud and thin as if each note leaps upward and mingles with the militant sky. The naked dancer is driven into a frenzy with her body having become fluid, moving in one with the drums, the chanting.

The low haloed moon disappears behind clouds that lend the warm night a deep frustrated darkness. The star-studded blanket above loses its luminescence as the stars slide behind advancing pregnant masses. Far away thin silver cracks define the darkened sky, followed by a long low grumbling. The release comes. Riding on the tail end of one primal growl of thunder the sky falls down in strong fat drops. The dancer is spinning round and round with arms lifted high above in the age-old gesture of supplication. The rain lashes at her body, joins with her sweat and gasping breath and finally enters the ground at her feet. Panting still, and chest heaving up and down, she comes to a stop facing the onslaught of the rain. She sinks to her knees and listens...

I wake.

My eyes are wet with tears, my body clammy from the heat. The prescient aroma of damp soil tickles my nose. I sneeze, then lie very still. Lightning steals into the room, briefly chasing all the shadows out. Retreating in a flash the room is again cloaked in heavy darkness. A low rumble shakes the air and the ground, making the house shift on its foundation and the windows rattle. It is the kind of thunder that sends cockroaches scurrying for cover.

Like the labour pangs and groans of a woman about to deliver, the lightning traverses the sky in hot laser flashes answered by deep sonorous thunder that demands attention. A vicious bolt trips timid car alarms into a clanging that adds to the din.

The first sharp drops hit the asbestos roof in a quick, hard patter lasting about fifteen heartbeats. Then absolute silence. I hold my breath, suspend my thoughts. A loud bang, and the rain comes.

I have a primal love of storms. I want to revel in the power of the raging elements. I want to throw my arms up into the pulsating air. I want to hurl myself into the din and shout and scream and clap and stomp. I have only done that once, once in the days of my youth among the hills and mountains of home. I rode the storm, and became one with the elements. It was one of those sacred moments in my life, a baptism. I was cleansed.

I slide out of bed and stand at the window to watch the storm. It is the first rain after a long drought.

It comes down angry and challenging, whipping the houses, the skeletal trees and the hard dry ground with sullen savagery. Strong currents blow this way and that way, sending the lashing sheets in all directions as if insisting on scouring every surface.

It is a rain to wash away all the corruption in the land. A rain to cleanse and restore all that has been touched by the dark side of man. It is a rain so powerful that it first has to rage and blow, punch and pummel, and flash and flood to flush out all that has poisoned our lives.

The first rains. A cleansing. I remember Gukurahundi. A time of loss and degradation. One man's moment of madness. Gukurahundi, a beautiful word, to crown man's depravity. My thoughts will not go that way. I shall not let them. I shall put the lid tight on a wound that will not heal.

The first rains. I remember Murambatsvina. I still see the children in soggy rags standing beside mangled remains, sticking out from the muddy ground, of the only home they ever had. Where shall they shelter, those whose homes were demolished? Unsightly? Yes. Hovels? Yes. Poor? Yes. Landless? Yes. But how did this come about in a land of the free? How did they get there? Murambatsvina; another cleansing to hide our shame and our shortcomings. But the poor will not be exterminated.

The first rains. A cleansing. Business and banking. We have lost count of the false starts, failed operations, sunrises turned to sunsets. The economy breeds more hunger, more queues, more corruption. A cleansing that has spawned millionaire beggars and a billionaire middle class. Paper money with more zeros than can fit on a cheque.

I am spent. I am hollow. I am ready to dream, to fill up my mind with hope because without hope tomorrow is stillborn.

"Come back to bed, you witch. One of these days you will be struck by lightning. I am not ready to be a widower yet," Mandla's voice floats through the dark space from the bed.

It is a dream.

She is moving through green mealie fields. The stalks are heavy with giant cobs that trail with a long rich purple beard. In the background a jingle from the national broadcaster is playing softly, climaxing with the proclamation 'Mother of all agricultural seasons'.

Across the valley tractors and combine harvesters gleam in the smiling sunlight. They repose in orderly abandon like satisfied workmen viewing the fruit of their labour.

Rubbing shoulders with the machinery are cattle, goats and sheep grazing on the lush grass. Their heads occasionally leave the ground as if to comment to a fellow grazer on the richness of the meal.

In the manner of all dreams she is transported to another place where she finds herself filling up a glass with a sparkling liquid, cool and clear, gushing out from the tap. She finds herself opening water taps that keep springing up everywhere. Through the sound of a thousand gushing taps she hears the turbines of Kariba whirring at a mighty speed and she knows it is the end of power cuts.

With her sharpened vision she takes in the heavily hung mangoes and peaches and guavas decorating the square yards in front of equally square houses.

The trees start shaking, the ground is shaking, shaking...

My eyes pop open.

"Mom, wake up, wake up. The taps are coughing. Get the containers. We are going to have water. Wake up."

"It rained last night," I say with a smile.

"What?"

"It rained last night, " I repeat. "Everything is going to be all right."

My daughter looks at me oddly.

I keep on smiling.

LOOKING FOR THE SOUTHERN CROSS

Peter Finch

Looking for the Southern Cross wasn't easy
Lonli our guide, a Jehovahs, said god was in
all things including Bulawayo but he had
no idea. Try town. Natural History Museum full of
tired lions but no planetarium. The guard said cross
boy you want Jesus. Maybe I did. In the Alabama Club
where Jays Marabini and his Kozekulunge Jazzers
hammed it with red and blue shirted jive dancers
showing teeth like diamonds no one knew.
In the sky I counted three crosses. God
on southern overdrive. Outside the bottlestore the
touts and layabouts wore crucifixes. Old habit.
Robert Moffat started all this coming here from Ormiston
in 1859 with a bag of bibles. There's
a faded shot of him and his wife somewhere looking
like mill workers about to become holy sunbeams. Southern Cross
pulled him. Hard. He gave the Ndebele ground nuts, Jesus
and workless Sundays. God's done them proud.
The night sky is huge and unmasked
full of milky clusters of unpolluted light.
Beyond the centre the townships shake and suffer
no god, no planning, homeless under the bastard cross,
chased by a minotaur with no civilization.
Moffat bring back your singing. On the streets
they don't. The Southern Cross is up there by
the Coalsack but no one looks.

INNOCENCE

Ian Rowlands

I picked up the *Sunday Mail* that had been thrust under my bedroom door. On the front page there was a promise – 'The wheat harvest will not fail'. Somehow I knew it would. Such an assurance would not need to be set in bold print if the harvest was to be truly bountiful in the 'breadbasket of Africa'. In the lift down to the hotel lobby a Zimbabwean businessman mourned the rape of a fair country. "Zimbabwe was fruitful," he said. "It's now barren... destroyed." The night before, in conversation with an elderly white woman, the subject turned to suicide. "The black rat poison is best, it has higher levels of strychnine." She paused, not for effect; possibly from the memory of buying a box. "We are also Zimbabwean... African. But we are no longer welcome here. After three decades working on the railway, my husband's monthly pension does not even buy a loaf of bread! We can't stay here, but we can't afford to leave." Even if the wheat harvest was to be as bountiful as the paper promised, she, for one, would not be able to afford the bread it would be used to bake. My breakfast that morning cost more than the Zimbabwean average weekly wage.

An hour later. "Before you leave, I want to take you to a high density suburb," our host said as we got into the four by four outside the Rainbow Hotel. Wearing *Ray Bans*, I joined the rest of the party as we drove to the outskirts; white hunters with cameras. I recalled the American hunters at Bulawayo's Joshua Mqabuko Nkomo Airport who flashed their high velocity rifles before customs officials; pointing their barrels in our faces as they looked for registration numbers. "Can you carry hand guns in Zimbabwe?" a Texan drawled. "Yes, for reasons of legitimate self defence," his safari guide assured him. "Good. What's the going rate for a lion? Ten thousand... twenty thousand US?" What's the going rate for a Texan?

We drove along roads lined with people selling a single car part, a few tomatoes, their souls for a fist full of dollars more. The night before we'd paid for our pizzas with a Twin Tower of notes and took pictures of ourselves laughing at tumbling absurdity.

"It's Monopoly money," we joked to the till operator.

"It's not money... it's no game," came the rejoinder.

Shot down, we nodded with understanding, understanding nothing. "Coffee?"

Unexpectedly we turned into a compound on the very edge of the city. "We're stopping here for tea," our host explained.

"Why?" I asked.

From inside the vandalised hut a few children emerged. "This is an orphanage we are trying to support for children who have lost both their parents to AIDS." Inside the four by four there was silence; the last few moments of security before we faced up to the reality from which we, as a cultural delegation, had hitherto been shielded.

Granted, there was that conversation in a Cape Town restaurant: "I gave my son a cell-phone for his twenty first birthday."

"Nice," I said.

"He was travelling on a train; never use the trains."

"Sure," I responded, reaching for the gnocchi.

"When he was assaulted by a gang who wanted to steal his phone."

"Oh, no..."

"But he fought them off."

"Oh, great."

"He'd grazed his knuckles. He went to the doctor, now he's HIV positive. Any more pizza?"

That, and apart from the odd anecdote ("We sell vegetables in the market. We can always tell those who are HIV because they buy all the beetroot."), and government quackery in the media, AIDS hadn't touched our visit. Perhaps we'd all walked down the street wondering, which one in every three? It's safer if we avoid everybody. So that's what we did. No better than the blind eyed governments, I guess. As we walked into the hut, around forty children, aged between one and fourteen, sang and danced. They sang hymns of hope; hymns that promised a better life than the one they were leading. Few of these children would have healthy years ahead of them, and I, a white atheist with a purse ample enough to be cynical, had no right to question their hope. 'God has left Africa' someone once wrote. It is ironic that while God has left Africa, God is omnipresent in the West where God is needed least. "Oh God," choked in my throat.

"Don't cry," my host whispered, "crying solves nothing."

Forty children looked after by one woman. Forty smiling children; their joy, the most precious gift they could ever give.

When they had finished singing for us, a colleague turned to me, "Sing Ian," he urged.

"Sing?" I asked.

"Please. You can speak Welsh, for God's sake sing."

From the age of fourteen I have stayed silent in churches and chapels for every hymn. As a man I sing once a day, and once a day only. "This is a song," I began, "This is a song I sing to my son... my son, each night before he goes to sleep... It is a Welsh song called *Ar hyd y nos* – All through the night."

As I sang, I pictured my son's little head on his pillow listening to his dad singing him to sleep. "Shhh, Caspar. No more questions... we'll talk Star Wars in the morning.... *Golau arall yw tywyllwch, i arddangos gwir brydferthwch*...." Darkness is another light, which illuminates true beauty.... Forty orphans listened as I sang a son's lullaby from 'another country'.

After tea, squash for the children, I talked football with a group of boys.

"My name is Ian. What's yours?" I asked a boy of about eight.

"Innocent," he said. "My name is Innocent..."

He smiled. I smiled as I knew immediately that, as a writer, he would be the seed of a story; words upon a page, a moment of intense irony, a moment I would drag out to illuminate a point.

"Nice name," I said, "Innocent..." As I write this, I can see your face, Innocent. And I wonder, as I consider your Zimbabwe from a distance, what manner of man would allow such innocence to be destroyed? Guilty of nothing but hope.

Half an hour after our uneasy goodbyes, we were eating panini and drinking lattes in an affluent suburb; tall gates to keep out the poor and the 'innocent'. Four hours later we were wasting time in Johannesburg's OR Tambo International Airport. I bought elephant shorts for my son, trying to get rid of the spare rand in my pocket; a lifetime's pension for an ex-railwayman in distant Bulawayo. Twenty four hours later, I was home and singing my son to sleep once again.

"Last night I sang this song for little boys and girls in Bulawayo," I said.

"They have no mummies and daddies."

"Who sings them to sleep?" he asked.

"No-one," I replied.

"Oh…"

"Don't cry, Caspar."

Crying solves nothing.

JUSTICE

Wim Boswinkel

"Always complaining," complained Phil Chibaya, "just count your blessings and see how lucky you are." The man opposite him tried to force a smile on his thin face. He was not hungry as in starving, but could do with a meal. His last one had been eighteen hours ago, if you could call it a meal when there was no relish. It had been at home, with just enough sadza for him and his family to satisfy their bodies' most urgent needs; for who could be concerned about proteins and vitamins these days?

Chibaya, a heavy balding man, well into his fifties, was seated in a high-backed leather chair at a large teak desk. Behind him was the usual photograph of the Old Dictator in which he still looked quite serene, as it was taken in the early nineties, when his hands were relatively clean.

Phil stared intently at a pornographic picture on the screen of his laptop (strategically placed so as not to give away to visitors that he was actually not *working* on it), while, with an indifferent gesture, handing the man a bundle of freshly printed banknotes, the nominal value of which could have bought half the city a few years earlier. Now it would be just enough for twenty kilos of mealie meal, which would only be available at the end of a long queue of dehumanized people in some back alley.

Another young girl appeared on the screen, revealing all of her thin white body. Phil had already forgotten his caller, who was now leaving the office. Why should he give him a second thought, after all, he had been quite generous in not just laying him off without a cent. With his political connections, he could easily have got away with that. But then he had been an active church member all his life.

51

As life-sized pudenda appeared on the screen, beads of perspiration sprouted on his big gleaming head. It was not the only part of his body affected. He sighed, wiped his face with an Air Singapore tissue (first class) from his last shopping trip and switched off the laptop; it was still too early to follow up in the flesh.

There had been no load shedding that morning and apparently no faults either, since the robots 'worked' at the intersection of Seventh and Spring Avenues, giving Nontokozo a chance to sell a few airtime cards to drivers who had to stop anyhow.

It was clear that not only doctors, engineers and teachers had left the country in the ongoing brain-drain; they must have been joined by the person who was responsible for adjusting the lights and replacing the bulbs. Orange did not function in three of the four robots, but, as if to compensate, stayed on for almost half a minute in the one where it did. In another two robots green was not working and red had broken down in one of the four. And, as if that was not enough, Seventh Avenue, which is much busier than Spring Avenue, had far shorter green periods than the latter.

Nontokozo was a slight girl, who looked sixteen, although she would be twenty in a few months. She had made a living at this corner for more than four years, ever since she had had to drop out of Form Four. A year before that sad occurrence, her father had lost his job at the National Furniture Factory, after Phil Chibaya had bought it and sold off its assets. Almost a quarter of a century of faithful work had come to nothing.

In the first year, the family lost their house as they were unable to pay the rent, while a year later, all five children had to leave school as their parents were unable to pay the school fees or to buy the uniforms. But 2007 had been the worst year. One morning some neighbours found her father hanging from a tree, and, a couple of months later, her elder sister died of AIDS. She had not been able to get the anti-retrovirals, which were only available to the well-connected few.

From then on, she also had to earn money for the upkeep of her sister's baby and, as her commission from airtime sales was not enough, she eventually had to accept, once or twice a day, the invitations of passing drivers. It went against all that she believed in and made her feel dirty, but she had little choice but to give in to their demands, in their cars or in cheap rooms.

Her hatred for Chibaya had turned into an obsession of late. She could not avoid seeing him regularly on television and in the papers, where he was featured as one of the country's most successful businessmen, an example to follow. And on many a night, lying on the mat that she shared with two sisters and the baby, she was kept awake by the vision of his face.

Two weeks ago she recognized him behind the steering wheel of a silver *BMW*. The car slowed down as it turned into Spring Avenue, stopped 50 metres from the corner and hooted. This was the standard way in which she was approached by men who were not interested in airtime.

Trembling and with a heavy heart, Nontokozo walked up to his car. When he lowered the window she could feel the escaping cold air. It was him, that repulsive person who haunted her day and night, the man who had destroyed her family and her future.

"What else are you selling, girl?"

They were all the same. Almost all the men used that phrase.

She shivered, she felt frozen inside, but she gave him the smile that was her usual answer.

"I will see you sometime," he said while handing her some banknotes. Then he took off.

The coke and pie that she bought with it tasted tainted, but she was hungry.

Phil Chibaya got up from his desk and walked out of the office into a wide corridor. All the other rooms were empty, even the carpets had been removed. He walked into a large factory hall, where two workers were packing the disassembled parts of the last two spinning machines that had been bought by an entrepreneur somewhere over the western border. He had paid Phil in hard currency and paid well; this had been a modern spinning mill with the latest technology.

Chibaya had used this profitable procedure many times. It started with his political friends getting a company in trouble; they stopped allocating foreign currency for fuel and machine parts, and the company would only be paid in local currency for its export-sales at an artificial rate that only represented a fraction of the real value. Suddenly it would start making big losses. The final blow was then delivered by Phil's friends in the ministry selling import licenses for cheap Chinese goods to other political associates, causing the internal market to collapse too.

The almost bankrupt company would then be put up for sale by its desperate owners and some bogus bank, stacked with freshly printed cash, would issue a loan to Phil Chibaya to purchase it. He would lose no time in firing the personnel and in looking for a buyer for the machines and the remaining stock.

Each time it had been as simple as that. Another few million US dollars would be deposited into his overseas account. And, if the bogus bank still existed, the repayment of the loan after a year would amount to almost nothing as his political cronies would see to it that the country's inflation rate grew by thousands of per cent in the meantime.

Phil was thinking about the girl that he had been ogling on the laptop. He liked them young, but for a white girl he would have to wait for his next trip to Europe; today the little phone girl would have to do.

It would be pay-back time for her; twice in the last two weeks he had handed her some money. She should certainly be expecting him.

Throwing a last glance at the empty factory hall, he moved towards the gold *Cadillac* that he had picked for this day. He put the laptop on the seat next to him and started the engine.

Life is good, he thought, as long as you stick to the rules. He had always been a law abiding citizen, never stole, never raped, never killed anybody. Of course, righteous people like him should be able to reap the benefits. For a brief moment he thought of the man who he had paid off earlier in the office. Loser, he shrugged off the memory, what did he expect? Lucky for people like him that there are the likes of me!

He switched on his CD-player and joined in, loudly singing Lucky Dube's last song – the poor bastard, he had deserved better.

Nontokozo had not sold a single airtime card that morning. There had been no power since last night, causing the traffic to flow past in an orderly fashion, simply following the rule of giving way to the right. She was bemused by the fact that working robots often caused chaos, rather than smoothing the traffic through. Sitting on her log in the shade of a jacaranda tree, she had plenty time to think.

She was quite a philosophical girl, who loved reading. Things tended to balance themselves out, she realized. Yes, there were more potholes than ever, but the same misrule that was responsible for not maintaining the country's infrastructure also caused the lack of fuel and the resulting reduction in the number of cars running around. There was no longer electricity and paraffin to cook with, but at the same time the breakdown of the rule of law had seen to it that plenty firewood was available from vandalized farms. God had not completely forgotten the country, she concluded.

The first car of the morning stopped around the corner in Spring Avenue. "Sorry, not today," she shouted to the surprised driver.

The baby had finished the last of the milk that morning and she was almost broke, but she did not want to lose the opportunity she had waited for so long. She wanted to be there when Phil Chibaya came for her. He had passed again the other day and given her more money. Nontokozo guessed that next time he would expect her to go with him. She dreaded that moment, but at the same time was determined and ready. She could feel the long metal spike through the imitation leather of her bag.

It took another two hours, and one more disappointed client, before the conspicuous *Cadillac* approached the junction of Seventh and Spring Avenues.

She clutched her handbag tightly and walked to the vehicle. Opening the door on the passenger side, she eased herself on to the seat from which Phil Chibaya had removed his laptop.

The icy temperature made her feel better and, by the time he turned his car into the lonely farm road, she was in full control of herself.

East Park cemetery lies along the road that leads to the Great Falls. Dark clouds were gathering in the sky as the funeral got underway. It was attended by hundreds of people. Almost all the cabinet was there, headed by the Vice-President. Jane Chibaya had just arrived in time from London where she had been shopping; most of her children who studied abroad had also made it to what would be their father's last resting place.

The ceremony was led by the Archbishop himself, a very humane being. The usual long obituaries were delivered, tears were shed, prayers were offered and hymns were sung.

As the coffin was lowered, the Archbishop glanced away towards the road to the Great Falls. There were no cars to be seen, tourism was dead in the failed country.

But there is hope, the holy man thought, the rains are near and should be above average, according to the meteorologists. There might even be food again in a couple of months.

He noticed that the coffin had reached the bottom of the freshly dug grave. A lamenting hymn started up, the women taking the lead.

And, thought the prelate, even the Old Dictator cannot destroy the Great Falls; one day the tourists will be back. He smiled while he visualized a new country with honest leaders and happy, healthy, free, well-fed people. He felt inspired, raised his arms and uttered a blessing.

The sun has completely disappeared behind a thick layer of clouds.

Nontokozo is back at her road junction.

She is a different person. Inside, she feels relaxed and at peace with herself. Outside, she looks good, the sale of the laptop having realized enough money to enable her to buy attractive clothes and some make-up and to have her hair extended with hundreds of tiny playful braids. Surely more cars would now stop in Spring Avenue.

That late morning with Chibaya had been the climax of her mental and physical torment. His climax gave her the opportune moment to carry out what she felt was her duty to her family and herself. That act had liberated her as she knew it would. From now on, she could look after her dependents without constantly thinking of the past. She could live with herself and look forward to the many good things that life still had to offer.

The first raindrops start to fall; she happily unfolds her new umbrella.

MY COUNTRY

Julius Chingono

My country is like
an empty but attractive
plastic packet
marked in bold blue letters
fresh creamy milk
being blown by the wind
along the road
that leads to a rubbish dump
by the cemetery.

KING OF BUMS

Christopher Mlalazi

The lecture room is packed tight.

"I want to warn you," the Minister says in a dragging voice. "Please, never ever make the mistake of looking down on us. We freed this country," he points at us. "We freed you, and now you think we are stupid."

My hand shoots up, and the Chair, reluctantly, points at me. I know he does not like me, or should I say my liberated mouth, which is quite famous around the campus. The remote mike is passed over to me by an usher.

"Minister," I begin to a hushed room. Black and white heads are twisted back at me from the chairs, as I am standing at the back of the room, just by the door. "What pains me the most about war veterans is that they seem to think that, since they freed the country, we who did not go to the war owe them our lives." The Chair is scowling at me, and the white haired Minister's teeth are bared in a fixed smile. "They fail to grasp that, if we had been old enough at that time, we could have done what they did, and just as well too."

The usher reaches for the mike, but I brush his hand away. I continue. "We ask them to respect us as we respect them by not continuously reminding us of the war – that is history now. We should be looking forward, seeking ways on how we can unite the diverse peoples that make up this country, and, most importantly, how we can rejuvenate the country to make it the bread basket of Africa once more, instead of the basket case it has been reduced to because of political incompetence."

The usher's hand darts in from below and snatches the mike away.

I remember their colourful return from the bundu. I was still very young then, at that tender age when kids take delight in tailing amorous couples into the bushes behind the township for a free porno, or peep through chinks in curtains in lodgers' bedroom windows at night.

I remember the women the most. *Wena!*

A gramophone was set on a chair outside a house behind our line, belting out intoxicating rumba, and these two women, in guerrilla camouflage, were, of all things, screwing the air in time to it, and all so beautifully done!

That dance, called *skokocha*, imported from foreign freedom fighter camps, was pregnant with meaning. It promised the birth of new and exciting things for the country. It augured riches for us poor township dwellers, who lived in crowded houses with no electricity, shared communal water taps and who crapped in smelly pit latrines, where, if you dared peep down the pit, you could see the fat maggots wriggling in the shit.

But seen from this lofty thirty four that I possess today, it also promised a later screwing of the masses by politicians who said do this with one hand, while they did that with the other – just like shameless itinerant magicians.

Life was one hell of a big adventure then. *Toyi toying* under the silver stars at night around the townships with the victorious guerrillas, openly insulting whites, our oppressors then, with no threat of youth militia bombing the shit out of us, no riot police tear-gassing us, no cell doors clanging shut on us, no secret police tailing us – even no censorship. We were one big jubilant family, or so it appeared to me.

Amidst all this euphoria, for the first time, the store was robbed.

I was skipping along the street that autumn afternoon, feeling half guilty and half happy with myself. I had just nicked a tickey from home, and I was going to buy a sherbet from the store. If mama discovered the theft, well, there were three of us boys at home to suffer for it, even if the others were not going to see the sherbet. And as I was the youngest, I also knew that my punishment was not going to be as severe as the others' – sometimes I had also been beaten by mama for pennies I had not stolen; so what the hell!

Half way to the shops, a man flew from around a corner, running hard, and carrying a briefcase. It was the storekeeper! Two men in rice camouflage were chasing him, one wielding a hammer, and the other a long bladed knife. Strangely, no cheering onlookers followed this chase as is the habit of the township. I watched them disappear around another corner.

That evening, I heard father telling mother when he tottered in from the beer-garden that the store had been robbed by 'them'.

Other robberies followed, and the guerrillas assumed another exciting aura for me. At that time I was reading *Robin Hood*, and I liked to liken them to him. Robbing from the rich and giving to the poor. For hadn't they taken the country from the rich colonial regime and given it back to us? I also visualised them taking from the storekeeper again and giving to us, for then, being a storekeeper was being rich, and the storekeeper never gave anything away for free, instead, he sold, and those without money went hungry. Being a teacher was regarded as rich too then, not this farce of today where grossly underpaid and nearly destitute teachers borrow money from their students to try to make ends meet.

I loved to listen to mother and father talking in bed after the candle had been blown out at night. It was fluent talk that solidified the world and life for me, and often transported me to far away lands, to magical places in the rural areas where they had grown up and met. It was a revelation to me to learn who were witches amongst our relatives and neighbours. They also talked about politics, and I now doubt if they understood all that was happening, no matter how eloquently they seemed to express their opinions about it to my ears, for they had had little education. And, come to think of it, as close as I slept next to their bed, I never heard them fornicating, not even once. I remember one day asking mother where she had got the baby she came back carrying after a few days absence from home, and she had said she had bought it at the store.

Then Takemore, a neighbour's son, came back from the war after a four year absence. He became an instant hero to us kids.

In the evenings after supper, we would sit in a ditch on one side of the street, and he would fill us with awe inspiring stories about his bundu days that made me rue that I had not been born earlier so that I too could have crossed to the guerrilla camps. One such story was how one day he had been hiding in a cave from white soldiers who had been chasing his platoon, and a big snake had slithered over him.

"I spat at it and it died," he told us, much to our amazement. "If I had let it go it would have given away our position on the skin of the earth."

Takemore never associated with any adults, although he was adult himself, and had a beard and pubic hair. I saw the hair through the legs of his shorts one day when he was squatting on the ground as he made a wheel for my toy wire car, because he wore no underwear – and he had such big balls! He was always surrounded by us kids. He taught us press-ups, which he said he had learnt overseas. There was one that we could not perform, the two-finger one.

"Even your fathers and mothers can't do this one," he used to boast.

"Only a person who has flown in a Russian plane and slept with a white prostitute can."

He also taught us how to draw an AK-47 rifle in the dust, and then to make a wire model of it. There was one gun he talked the most about, which he said could shoot down even the sky if correctly aimed. He said it was so big that it needed four men to carry it – but he could carry it alone – and when it shot – *Heyi wena*! *Basop*!

"If you want to bring down the sky, shoot the sun," he told us. "But nobody can hit it, it's difficult because it is so far away, even *ntikoloshis* fail to reach it."

Then one day he told us he would be leaving the township very soon.

"I was promised a house in the suburbs by the Commander while I was in the bush," he told us in the ditch. He had just smoked *mbanje*, something I feared so much, even its smoke, because I had heard it said it could make one go crazy in the head and be taken to the asylum. "The white owners will be moving away soon. I also wanted the wife but the commander said no, we must leave the women alone, because war has rules and you just don't do things that the rule book says no to, like Idi did."

"Who is Idi?" I asked him.

"A black man who fucked Indian arses," he replied, stubbing the joint, then lighting a cigarette. "He drank human blood to get an erection for it." There were eight of us kids in the intimacy of the ditch, all boys. Takemore had passed the cigarette to me.

"Smoke," he encouraged. "Let's enjoy what the skin of the earth has to offer to comrades." I was eight then.

I took a pull, and passed the cigarette on. Finally it went back to Takemore, and he laughed as eight kids spluttered and coughed around him.

Then Gasa, who lodged in the house behind ours, walked past in the darkness.

"White boy!" Takemore called to him. Gasa leapt at him. They fought savagely, and people came out of the houses at the sound of the battle to watch, and they eventually separated them.

I heard father later saying to mother from their bed: "The gorilla wanted to kill the Selous Scout." That's how father pronounced guerrilla. But still, his pronunciation added to the allure of the guerrillas in my eyes, for I could now see a romantic figure clad in camouflage and armed with an AK-47 leaping from tree to tree in the jungle, helicopters chasing above, and white soldiers below.

61

While Takemore had disappeared before Independence, we had seen Gasa time and time again, coming home dressed in regime army camouflage, sometimes delivered in an army truck. I remember too one day, just before the ceasefire, when a haggard Gasa appeared from the bushes behind the township carrying a rifle, which I was to learn later had been an FN, with his uniform streaked with mud. He stayed in his house without coming out for two whole days. We waited hopefully for him to appear, for he often gave us delicious tinned food, especially me as he sometimes sent me to call various girls around the township for him whenever his wife was away in the reserves.

On the third night, he came out, bought a mug of *amasese* from the beer-garden and drank it with father in our house. While lying under the bed with my brothers, where we liked to play when there were visitors, also with the hope of hearing something juicy, I heard Gasa telling father that he had been involved in a fire-fight with terrorists.

"Don't tell me!" father exclaimed.

"I am the only one who managed to escape," Gasa continued. "I ran through the bundu for three days, and my first stop was here."

The following day, he went away wearing his uniform and carrying his rifle.

Then one sunset, just after Independence, father came back home looking glum. He did not speak to anyone, just took his chair and sat under the lemon tree, smoking roll-up after roll-up. We steered clear of him, for we were well familiar with this mood. Even mother avoided him. When darkness came, he was still sitting out there, and if one peeped out of the door, a tiny orange light could be seen under the lemon tree as he continued to smoke away whatever was bothering him.

Then later, in bed, I heard him tell mother.

"My whites have gone."

"*Hayi Ah!*"

"No more work for me."

"*Mayibabo*! Is this our dependence?" That is how she pronounced Independence. "No more jobs for our husbands?"

Up to that day, father worked as a 'garden boy' in a house in the suburbs, and he called his employers *amakhiwa ami* (my whites).

I remember them letting father push their baby boy in a pram along Moffat Avenue, while I ran happily along behind. I remember father scuttling on his hands and knees on the lawn of their front garden with this baby on his back, who was now and then hitting father on the buttocks with a stick and crying, "Girrup!" or something like that. This was such a happy picture for me...

Back home, I asked father if we could show mother the 'Girrup!' stunt he had performed with his employer's baby, and I received such a painful slap for my trouble.

Sometimes father brought us lovely toys from work. All of the toys were broken one way or the other, but as they say, half a loaf is better than none – kids came from far and wide in the township to play with the toys, elevating us to the status of celebrities. Then father started bringing us new ones. Beautiful little cars that you could wind up, place on the concrete floor, and they would zoom away on their own. Battery operated electric trains that, with a click of a switch, could transverse a miniature railway line, taking one on imaginary trips around the universe.

Then, one day, a man whom I recognised as working next door to father's whites came running home, his face covered in sweat. In a breathless voice, he talked to mother, and mother hastily took all the new toys to the house neighbouring ours. The man then went away. A few minutes later, a police jeep stopped in front of our house. Two black policemen, with father and the wife of his employer, Mrs Almstead, came out of the jeep and entered the house. I followed them in. One of the policemen was tall and the other fat and short. The policemen searched the room, and collected all the broken toys on the bed – we had no table. Then the tall policeman said something to the Madam in English – she shook her head, then she and the policemen smiled at a relieved looking father.

"The new ones are next door!" I cried out in Ndebele, wanting to assist, thinking they had come to admire the toys.

"Shut up!" the fat policeman snapped at me in the same language, but he was smiling, and he stroked my cheek.

The tall policeman asked the fat policeman something in Shona, his eyes, looking sharp, fixed on me. I did not understand Shona.

The fat policeman lifted me in his arms, smiled at the tall policeman, and replied to him in Shona.

Mother took me from the policeman's arms and carried me outside, but not before I noticed the murderous stare father directed at me.

"If you say anything to those policemen I will beat you!" she threatened, standing in front of the lean-to where she cooked our meals. "You are lucky the tall one does not understand Ndebele!"

I sensed that I had said something very wrong

Later, the group emerged from the house, all smiling at each other, father and Mrs Almstead included, and they all drove away.

"They personally told me they cannot be ruled by a kaffir," I heard father saying from the bed, the darkness in the room solid and threatening to sit on me and squash me flat to the floor. I was quizzing myself how, for we had sometimes bought chips from cafés in town – how could cafés rule people?

"They said that!" Mother's voice was shocked. "Then let them go with their jobs! We don't need them that much!"

As the country celebrated its new found independence, we celebrated our new found poverty. A now unemployed father became the township drunk, while mother, brave woman, went to the recently introduced adult literacy evening classes, and, during the day, sold vegetables at a street corner. Later, after passing her Grade Seven exam, she became a shop assistant in the local store, thus enabling her to pay our school fees. A year later, one excessively rainy day, father was found drowned in a flooded ditch, an empty bottle of Smirnoff in one jacket pocket and a dead rat in another – so I heard it whispered fearfully at the funeral wake. People believed that he had been bewitched. It was about that time that Takemore disappeared from the township too – for his new house in the suburbs, so I assumed. And O how I had envied him.

I am a lecturer at the university now because of the hard work of my late mother.

The well rounded Minister does not even bother to stand up to reply.

"We have heard about you university people," he says, assuming an expression which he thinks is dangerous. Maybe it was, once upon a time, when trees could do the bump jive and rocks could be pinched. "But just try it, we are waiting for you." His fat cheeks are shining like twenty thousand dollar *vetkoeks*.

Later that afternoon, as I wait in my old *405* at a red robot in the city centre, a ragged beggar, carrying a bulging sack over his shoulder, approaches my open window.

"Excuse me, comrade," he says through the window, smiling at me with stained teeth. He has a matted beard, and an offensive smell wafts into the car. "Can you please spare some coins for the poor – drought wiped me out in the resettlements."

I look at him, and gasp in surprise.

"Skin of the earth!" I cry out as I recognise him.

Behind him, the sky is clad in blue skin tights that threaten to burst at the seams and reveal the king of bums.

10 LANIGAN AVENUE

Mathew Chokuwenga

The rains had been endless, so had been his coughing. It had been days since I had been out to play. I missed driving my wire car around the white neighbourhood. The car I would bring alive with sounds that would erupt from my small mouth, *brum-brum*, *vam-vam*, *pee-pee*. I missed playing football with my friends, dribbling past them as if they were standing still. I was good at that, so good.

Outside the rains continued to pour down in a million silver strings. It was December, sometime between Christmas and New Year. My father was so sick – I had never seen him like that before, so desperate for life. He coughed once, then twice. I anticipated a third, but silence came instead. With such coughing I felt sure he was dying. Knocking on heaven's door. Yes, my father was heaven quality. How could a man like him miss heaven? He was like the Father Christmas of the whole neighbourhood. A living hero. Not that he had much, except of course for a big heart. A heart big enough to accommodate the world.

My father wasn't much, just a cook. Few opportunities came his way because he had had little schooling, keeping him a slave to life. He wandered from one white family to another. I can't remember how many white folks he had worked for; it's all he had done with most of his life. Wasted time I had always thought. Out of all the white people he had worked for, I only really knew one. One old lady, very much older than my father. I often thought she had exhausted her life and was living on extra time. Anytime soon she must be called home to rest.

Mrs Lanigan. She wasn't much in height. A mere one metre point four, or five at the most. From afar she looked white, but as she held my small hand and walked me around her flower garden she became pink. A pale pink. Her palms felt so soft. I think it was her age that caused that. Her skin was no longer tight, forcing wrinkles to form all over her. She loved to sing, especially to me. One I remember sounded like:

Fere shaka, fere shaka
Dori mevu, dori mevu
Sonile makina, sonile makina
Ding, dong, du
Ding, dong, du.

Maybe my favourite was:

Daisy, Daisy
Give me your answer do
I'm half crazy
All for the love of you
It won't be a stylish marriage
For I can't afford a carriage
But you'll look sweet
Upon a seat
Of a bicycle made for two
Pee, pee.

I was made to learn all these songs, until I could sing along with Mrs Lanigan word for word. It must have taken a lot of time and effort. Anyway, I did manage to lock most of them into my head. These times that she and I spent together paid off handsomely, especially when I enrolled in grade one. Just like that I became a genius in the English language. Totalizing all the exam papers. I think even the teachers envied me. When it came to these foreign words I was way ahead of the pack, thanks to Mrs Lanigan.

Mrs Lanigan knew a lot because she had seen a lot. World War I, featuring the ambitious Kaiser. World War II, featuring the very ambitious Hitler, and Hiroshima, which she called America's greatest evil. Who knows, perhaps she might even live to see World War III. But, in all the time I knew her, she never left 10 Lanigan Avenue.

My parents, myself, my two brothers and my two sisters all lived with Mrs Lanigan. Not in her big house of ten or so rooms where she lived all by herself, but somewhere behind it in a two roomed cottage. It was small for the seven of us to fit in, but fit in we did for much of my life.

I remember once the door being kicked wide open and Joseph, the oldest of us children, being dragged away. He had defied the Rhodesian call up. I guess he had seen no sense in fighting his own and for that he had been guilty. He left home soon after they released him and ran away. I was still very young then, too young to understand what was going on.

My father coughed again, I could feel his pain in me, in my bones, in my flesh, in my head and in my mind. Tearing me apart bit by bit. I walked from the window towards his bedroom. The bedroom door was not quite closed. I pushed it and it yawned wide open. There was my father lying on the bed. He tilted his head towards me, fighting to keep his eyes open.

"Maphew," he said. Why did he have to give me a name he could not pronounce? Maybe it was Mrs Lanigan who had named me; after all, she seemed to pronounce my name much better than my own father. But maybe it was my father after all, maybe he just ran into Mathew when he was reading his bible. I vowed to find out one day.

Father was now as thin as a reed. Trying to feed him didn't help, he couldn't eat enough to keep his bones buried under his flesh. At the hospital they said he had cancer, but my mother had begged to differ. "That's a woman's disease," she had parroted over and over again. I was just too young to understand any of that stuff.

Lanigan Avenue was long and straight, named, of course, after Mrs Lanigan. I guess she was a pioneer resident. On one of its sides jacaranda trees ran along the whole of its length. On the other side Hartley One Primary School stood neat and green. During weekends I would often stand by the school fence and watch the white kids play. Dragging each other down, pushing and pulling, then suddenly one of them would break away, running madly like an escaping convict, with an oval ball tightly held to his chest. The whole lot would then pursue him, becoming his tail in seconds. It was all about that ball – where it was, where it was about to go and who was going with it. It was all that mattered to them on that pitch. Later I learnt the sport went by the title rugby. I never did lust for that sport. I was more into girls' hockey and tennis. I surely made time for those. No doubt it was those short skirts that ballooned my appetite for those two games. It wasn't my fault, it was my age.

Mrs Lanigan referred to my father as 'Peter', and Peter was indeed one of the names on his ID. He addressed her as 'Madam'. 'Madam' this and 'Madam' that. Just like the army, 'Sir, yes Sir' or 'Sir, I am a fool Sir'. I never dared to call him by his first name or he would have sent me to the land of the dead without a return ticket.

Water is what I brought to him after a couple of minutes. I made the door yawn once more as I sped towards him with that cup of water as if it was the master medicine of life.

"Here, Father," I said with my small voice. He had not managed to keep his eyes open while I was gone. I placed his cup of water on the floor slightly below his head. I stared at him as he lay there and willed him to live. It was my love for him that drove me to think positively against all my fears. Erasing from my mind all those recurring images of his funeral, of all those wailing women. Ripping into pieces that brown coffin in my head.

Mr Ellis was a friend of Mrs Lanigan, maybe much more in the past. Whether it was Mr Ellis who loved flowers, or Mrs Lanigan who loved sending Mr Ellis flowers, I did not know. But most Saturday mornings she would patiently pick a bunch and ask me to take the flowers to him. I did not mind at all, because actually Mr Ellis and I were pretty good friends.

"Who is it?" he would answer my knock, dragging that who word a bit. I never bothered responding, for, within seconds, he would be by the door, adjusting his spectacles for a better look. At the same time, puffing and coughing on his black pipe.

"Oh, Mathew," he would say, directing me in with his vacant hand. His place was not that big. Three rooms – bedroom, bathroom and kitchen/sitting room. For a single man like him, I thought the rooms were more than enough. Like Mrs Lanigan, he never seemed to leave his home. He loved smoking, cigarettes as well as his pipe, and his rooms smelled of smoke. What I liked most about Mr Ellis was that, every time I made a flower delivery, he would handsomely reward my services. Sometimes with a silver five cent coin that had a hare on it, or sometimes with a ten cent silver coin with a baobab tree. What more could I ask? The other thing I liked about Mr Ellis was his blindness to colour. When I was with him we were like two white folks, or two black folks. Perhaps more like two white folks as we spoke his language, shared his food and listened to his weird opera music. My listening to his

69

opera music was not exactly through pleasure. He was starved of company, so my visits were special to him. Not that he said so exactly, but I could just tell. Greenways is what they called the old age home where Mr Ellis was spending the last days of his life, pretty much alone.

Despite my cup of water, my father passed on later that day with nothing to his name. Leaving us nothing.

PASSING VILLAGES

Anne Simone Hutton

Each hut would step from a mountain
shadow, would then release its shape back
into the mountains so that a link was
established between the villages and their
background. Each roof had a nippled top

which we lifted in our minds, to try
the darkness that was potted inside.
The people matched their homes. When
they walked they walked in a neat line
beside the road, the way embroideries

walk a tablecloth and don't walk beyond.
They did not have windows, and waved
from doors, from poles in gates, from racks
on which corn and grass were scattered to dry.
When our car had struck the rhythm

of the road the children began to dance;
tea cosy-skirted girls, boys with toys
in wire. They brought out their hands
to catch sweets and pens from the city;
they caught nothing but rays of sun and dust

spat by tyres. We, however, stopped to take
what fruit of theirs we might need.
And what had dropped from our tablecloths,
the women and children in stitched
pictures, was returned to the landscape.

A LAZY SUNDAY AFTERNOON

Monireh Jassat

It had been a few years since my Dad died. My mother, my sister and I had gone through much but were still standing and that was worthy of celebration. Propping us up along the way had been an extensive network of family and friends, all of whom had helped to lighten our load, lend a sympathetic ear, or simply jolly us along our, at times, dark and dreary way. So, in honour of our survival and in gratitude to the women who had been there for us, Mom decided to hold a Sunday afternoon tea at Nesbitt Castle. She phoned around to invite her mates, and everyone settled into eager anticipation of the event.

I awoke that Sunday morning with an unaccountable sense of unease. Instead of the anticipation of a pleasant afternoon mellowing my mood, there hung a heaviness and gloom I seemed unable to dispel. The sky outside my bedroom window was dull and overcast and the very wind seemed to be fretfully trying to shake off the ill that clung to it. I felt a shiver run down my spine.

Mom it seemed was not unaffected by the general malaise. She went about her Sunday tasks quietly with an edginess that made it clear she also felt something to be wrong.

As we got ready to leave in our faithful old *Mazda 323*, she did something unusual for her. "You drive," she said, holding out the keys to me.

It was not often Mom relinquished roles of command, and driving was one she usually firmly reserved for herself. As I avoided it whenever possible the situation suited us both perfectly.

"No thanks," I replied, pulling a face.

She gave me a curious look for a moment, then let out a sigh. "OK. Let's go," she said shrugging her shoulders.

Of the dozen or so of us meeting at the Castle, those living close to each other had arranged to share lifts to conserve precious petrol. Mom and I were to collect three friends who lived not far away from us in Suburbs. The two younger women kept an immaculate house with their elderly mother who had been widowed. They had been there for us through thick and thin and, having suffered their own close bereavement, knew instinctively when to say or do the right thing.

Arriving at their gate we hooted to signal our presence. Although it was mid-afternoon in a 'safe' part of Bulawayo, with many people around, we still took the precautions of keeping our doors locked and our windows shut for fear of hijackers. Hazar, the elder sister, arrived first and settled into the front seat of the car whilst I moved to the back. Fathia, the younger sister, was still completing some chores so we chatted amongst ourselves while waiting for her and her mother.

After some time, Mom decided to chase her up and, rolling down her window, stuck out her head and yelled: "Come on Fathia!" Laughing, she turned back to Hazar, only to be confronted with a look of pure terror on her friend's face. "Quick!" Hazar cried in panic. "Roll up your window. Those men are coming towards us."

Mom, turning back to see what was going on, found herself staring straight into a pair of bloodshot eyes, framed by a balaclava. Before she had time to think, the keys had been snatched from the ignition and two black leather gloved hands grabbed her by her shoulders and tried to yank her from the car. Her instinctive resistance was met with a fist slammed straight into her face.

What happened next was something I marvel at to this day. Tightly curling up her arthritic hands and with a look of stubborn fury on her face, Mom threw a punch right back. The hijacker, although momentarily stunned, returned with a second punch, only to be met with an equally solid reply by Mom, who was not going down without a fight. As the hijacker reeled back we managed to pull the door shut and lock it.

A small built little dumpling of a woman who loved the social whirl and pottering about in her garden, Mom had always been an effervescent counterpoint to our tall and formidable father. Whilst she threw herself heart and soul into every dimension of life, he would take a back seat, preferring instead to quietly watch activities unfold around him. As children we rapidly learnt where Mom barked Dad bit and we pushed our limits accordingly. So my shock at being hijacked now proved secondary to my amazement at my mother's completely out of character reaction.

Seeking an easier target, the hijacker and his accomplices moved round to Hazar's door, which they yanked open. Hazar, who had been holding a top A sharp for at least two minutes and was evidently a loss to the world of opera, hung onto her handle with all her might. As I slid across the back seat to help her pull shut and lock the door I made a mental note, if we ever got out of this alive, to entice her to join the Bulawayo Philharmonic Choir with me. She would make an excellent soprano.

Dashing over to Mom's side they again unlocked and tugged open her door. This time the hijacker was taking no prisoners and Mom was assailed with a volley of punches and kicks. As she crumpled back on the verge of losing consciousness I realised with cold fear that I was on the knife-edge of becoming an orphan. Having already lost my father I could not bear to lose my mother too. I stretched across her body to shield her from further harm and, as the muddied heel of the hijacker's boot landed painfully on my collarbone, I screamed: "You will NOT take my mother from this car!"

Encouraged by the temporary reprieve, Mom, thankfully still conscious, gathered what strength she had left and aimed a kick squarely at his balls. As he doubled back in pain, we pulled the door shut and locked it. "Start the engine," I yelled to her forgetting the keys had been taken. "Start the engine and drive. Quick!"

Mom turned her blood-smeared face towards me. Her lips were swollen and desperation was etched into every feature. She was clearly hanging in there with everything she had. "He's got the keys," she sobbed. "They've taken the keys."

In that moment I journeyed many years back to a history lesson of mine at the Bulawayo Convent. We had covered the work our teacher had set and with the time remaining had meandered through various topics of discussion, one of them being what to do if ever hijacked. "You see," explained one particularly streetwise student as we all listened attentively, "one of the first things a hijacker will try to get off you is the car keys. If they have those don't try to keep them out by hanging onto the doors, because chances are they'll be physically stronger than you and before you know it they'll be in. If you can get the doors shut, keep them locked by holding the locks down with your fingers, because then it becomes almost impossible to open the doors from the outside, even with the keys."

"Push the locks down!" I yelled. "Hold the locks down!"

As one person Mom, Hazar and I held the locks down for all we were worth. In the lull that followed, battered, bruised and bloodied, we blinked up at our assailants.

In addition to the lead, and most aggressive, hijacker, there appeared to be two or three others positioned around our car. All of them had their faces covered but were well dressed and could not have been past thirty. Aside from the main guy, who was definitely a bit 'mental' and possibly on something, the rest of them seemed surprisingly like normal blokes. I watched as one gave his nose a good pick as he waited for their leader to make his next move. It came soon enough.

"If you don't get out of the car," snarled the hijacker in well-enunciated English as he produced a gun, "I'm going to shoot you."

This did not have the desired effect. By now terrified of what would happen if he did get into the car, we were more determined than ever to stay out for as long as possible, preferring to risk being shot dead than possible abduction and whatever else might follow. We had all heard the tales of rape and murder that hijack victims had suffered and our lead guy was clearly crazy enough for us not to want to leave any aspect of our personal welfare to his good graces, or lack of them.

Fathia, who had been on her way to the car when we were attacked, had run back into the house and had presumably called for help. We knew if we just held on long enough, relief would come. Somehow I could not help but feel the hijacker would have met with greater success if he had approached things calmly instead of scaring us silly.

"Thoot," exclaimed Mom in defiance through her bloodied nose.

Taking a deep breath he pointed the gun at Fathia and her mother, who had come out of the house and were bravely standing at the gate.

"If you don't get out of the car I'm going to shoot them," he snarled.

"You can shoot us," said Fathia calmly, before we were forced to make a decision over her and her mother's life. "But we've called the police and they're on their way."

At that, what we could see of the hijacker's features contorted with frustration and rage. Summoning his henchmen, to our amazement and relief, he slunk away from our car, hissing back his hatred for us as he disappeared round the corner.

Spurred on by his retreat Mom flew out of the car after him. Her hair was on end, and blood was spattered all over the beautiful new lime green dress she had picked out for the occasion. Realising she would not be able to catch them by herself, she caught sight of a maroon *Cressida* in the roadway. "Catch them," she yelled to the driver. "Quick! They're getting away. Catch them!"

The amply built driver, who definitely was not short of his sadza and stew, looked at her in blank astonishment.

"Catch them," she yelled more urgently, stamping her foot. "They're getting away. Don't let them go!"

"OK, Mama," replied the driver laughing. "We'll go catch them. We'll go catch them now," and, still laughing, he drove off in the direction of the hijacker and his cronies.

Slowly the rest of us took stock of the situation. Fathia and her mother had rushed to check on Hazar, who, although not physically hurt, was quite shaken, a bit tearful and, rather hoarse. I had a few bumps and bruises – but Mom had sustained by far the worst of the attack and, together with severe bruising, was quite badly bloodied.

She was also furious.

Displaying remarkable promptness, a grey van with armed police and dogs arrived a few moments later. As they got out, Mom rushed up to them to tell them about the attempted hijacking and how important it was they find the maroon *Cressida* that had gone to find the crooks. She was determined that as much as possible be done to catch the people who had so badly violated her person.

At the mention of the maroon *Cressida* the kindly faced officer in charge frowned. "Where was this car?" he asked cautiously. She explained it had been in the street at the time of the attempted hijacking. "That," he said shaking his head solemnly, "was the getaway car."

Loving the Self

Bhekilizwe Dube

He almost killed her. That's what it had to take. Near death. I still find it hard to understand why she put up with that abusive fool of hers for that long. Near death. That's what it had to take. I swear silently. If mom were still alive, this would have finished her.

"Is it always this bad?"

"This is nothing."

"Shit, it's tough here."

"Yeah."

"Nothing works here."

"Nothing."

"It's like this the whole day?"

"Yeah."

"Shit!"

"Yeah."

We are walking towards a winding queue at the local borehole. There are all sorts of containers, gallons, buckets, even the occasional dish and jerry can. Most of the people are badly dressed; they have poverty-darkened skins, skins tight and tense with poor nutrition. They are not shoving and pushing; they just shuffle to fill gaps in the queue. There are children at the borehole. These are lively and active. They run about, push each other around, shout at the top of their voices and laugh as if all is well. Most have swollen bellies typical of malnourished children. They are unaware of the poverty that is sapping the spirit and will of their elders.

I hate this sight. I can't stand seeing such passive and resigned poverty. I never come for water when there are queues by day. I fetch our water at midnight when most are asleep and there are no queues.

"Let's get away from this."

"You sound angry. It can't be helped if it's not raining properly, only God can help on that one."

"You sound like so many here, 'only God can help', 'the ancestors are angry, that's why it's not raining', 'the white god is angry because the whites have been mistreated here', 'the whites have gone with their money and with the rain'. You won't believe what Uncle Jabu says about all this!"

"What does he say?"

"He says that the whites are gods and they are angry, they will destroy everything if they don't get their farms back. He says nothing can work without them, they are gods of money and science."

"What do you think?"

I smile, her look is teasing when she asks. She knows how passionate I am about everything. She knows that things are much more complex than most people think. She wants to get me going. I don't want to get going. More than anything, I wish to get her going, wish to hear her side of the story, wish to know why it had to take a knife cutting into her to wake her up to something as obvious as that that fool did not love her. I respond reluctantly.

"It's global warming. The excesses of the white gods and goddesses in the western world are denying us rain. People don't seem to realise that things are interconnected in this world, that whatever happens anywhere at all on this globe affects us all one way or the other."

"Yeah. Most people here are still peasant farmers, they don't have the education or the energy to think about wider issues."

"Sure, they are still hewers of wood and breeders of children, that's why the politicians have a field day here, hell, in all of Africa. They are ruling people with a peasant psyche, they cheat them blind."

"You are going all passionate again, taking things personally, why does it matter so much to you?"

She has the look she always has when I care about things she thinks are better ignored, things like poverty, global warming, things like hollow politicians full of hollow ways and doings, things like humans loving to dominate fellow humans and giving them a tough time, hell, so many things, so many things.

I want to shout at her, shout that it's because of her casual attitude to things that she fails to see what they truly mean. I want to shout that it's such casualness that almost led to her death. How could she stand the touch of a man who hit her? How could she take being a punch bag for three years? How could she cook a meal for a man who had kicked her and strangled her before locking her out in central Johannesburg. How could she? It's her bloody casualness about the serious things of life that will be the death of her.

I look at her. I think of the poverty-stricken people in the queue. I think of her husband, that fucking vicious fool, may he collapse and die.

"Everything matters, everything is serious." That's all I can say.

We walk in silence. The queue is far behind us. All around are township houses, ugly things, creations of poverty. Only a few of them have any beauty.

"That's a nice house!"

Her exclamation is filled with joy. My sister loves beautiful things. For someone so aware of beauty I am saddened that she had wasted so many years in an ugly relationship, so many wasted years. Where is the beauty in being bashed? In being sworn at and humiliated? Where is the beauty in kicks, in slaps? Damn.

"I said that that house is lovely."

"Yeah."

"What's wrong with you, you love beautiful things."

"Yeah, I do, it's just that the house loses its beauty because it is drowning in a sea of ugly houses. Just look around you at all these houses; they look so grey with their unpainted walls, so dull with their unpainted grey asbestos roofs. What's the good of one beautiful house in a mass of ugliness? Why aren't the other houses beautiful as well, why must some have while others don't? Just imagine what this place would look like if all the houses were as beautiful and gay as that one? My imagining is nicer than what I see, so, I ignore what I see and live in my imagination."

She sighs, "You haven't changed."

"It's a harsh world."

"That's how things are."

"That's how we insist it must be, all is a product of imagination. In our minds, we imagine this ugliness, that's why we create it."

"Come on, this is reality."

"Reality is thought first, it's imagination first, it is dream first, then it takes solidity."

"Dreamer."

Perhaps if she had dreamt with her whole heart and mind of having a loving relationship with a caring man, she would have been drawn to such a man; if the dream is intense enough and serious enough, it assumes a life of its own and it seeks to be realised.

"You have gone into the clouds again."

"Not the clouds, I was in my mind, it's vaster than any clouds."

"We've gone far enough, let's go home."

"Yeah."

It's getting dark now. The dullness of the township is losing its glare now that the sun is setting. People walk about, children are playing, the fires are smoking, there is the inevitable power cut. Now and then an ugly car drives by; very rarely is the car a late model and beautiful. Some people are carrying hoes, they are from the maize fields they cultivate at the edge of the township. Peasantry refuses to die in the blood of these township dwellers. The fields they till are not very large, so many share them. Certainly, these urban peasants dream of larger fields to till, larger harvests and more abundant rainfall.

What are the dreams of urban dwellers in America, in Britain, in Japan?

"I am glad I came home."

She takes my hand. I smile. She is smiling too.

"Love yourself, Thandi."

"What do you mean?"

"When you love yourself, you seek the best for yourself, you don't put your body, your psyche, your mind and your heart through abuse."

She is quiet. She looks away. We are still holding hands. Still walking home.

"You don't have to have a man at all costs. Love yourself and dream wonderful dreams for yourself and cling to these dreams, don't give them up. Promise?"

"Promise."

We shall be home soon.

MISS PARKER AND THE TUGBOAT

Bryony Rheam

She was always an object of some interest, Miss Parker. Only because she wasn't married and at least forty-five, although back then, when everyone older than us was really very old, we imagined her to be fifty, sixty even, and that made her position even more questionable.

Rumour had it that she had been jilted at the altar, Miss Havisham-style, but, instead of occupying a big, old house and never taking her wedding dress off, she had decided to become a school teacher, a strict one at that, and scare the living daylights out of young girls with one stony stare or hard faced grimace from across the room.

She kept her greying hair short; it was of a cut best described as 'shower and go'. It was never blow-dried or combed differently, nor did it even have a smidgen of gel rubbed through it. She was big, not fat, but hefty. She wasn't the sort to eat her way through boxes of chocolates or have a standing order for cream buns at Haefeli's. Her longings, if they were there at all, were too well hidden to succumb to such temptations, for she was one who upheld sensible living above all else and everything in moderation.

She wore great ballooning trousers in navy blue and bottle green and white long-sleeved shirts and lace-up shoes and even a tie on the odd occasion. No jewellery, except a large brown watch and a Medic Alert bracelet. For some peculiar reason, she often wore a hat, a little white sailor's hat that she cocked to one side of her head and that we all found quite hilarious. Tugboat Thomas we'd call her and fall about laughing.

Someone said she used to be quite pretty, beautiful even, with long blonde hair and a golden brown tan and everything else that heroines possess in teenage romance novels. I'd imagine her standing at the altar, waiting excitedly for her love to arrive, her nervousness and then growing anxiety at why he was late. Had there been an accident? Was he all right? And then the news, the terrible life-changing news that he had gone. Eloped with someone else, or fled to France, or been put in prison for tax evasion. Something like that, and how her whole life changed, how she cut her hair and never ever wore make-up and dressed like a man so that no one could ever get near her and hurt her again.

Or perhaps he *had* been killed and she swore she'd never love anyone else. I pictured a heartbroken Miss Parker throwing a rose on her dead fiancé's grave, or flinging herself onto the coffin, willing her heart to break so she could join him, so they could be together forever.

Later, when we got tired of this idea, we believed for some time that she was a lesbian. To us, this explained the unfeminine clothes and manly walk, the gruffness, too, and the despising of all things 'girly'. When Janet Oatman almost drowned and Miss Parker performed CPR on her, we all looked at each other in acknowledgement, for our worst fears, we believed, were confirmed.

She was different to all the other teachers. There were, of course, those who weren't the most attractive of women, like Mrs Rose, but even she used to wear lipstick on consultation day and have her hair blow-dried for speech night.

Miss Ndlovu arrived when we were in form four and caused quite a stir. She had the most beautiful clothes and never wore the same thing twice in one term. Everything matched from her outfit to her jewellery to the nail polish on her toes. Even her watch had different straps that could be fitted to blend in with what she was wearing and we would watch in fascination as to what the next day would bring. She is the only teacher I have ever known who could look beautiful and cool last lesson on a Friday in October, when most of us were wilting in the heat, slumped across our desks, feeling little trickles of sweat run from our armpits. We were sure she had a long-term boyfriend, a fiancé even, although she was often sighted with various men and no one specific could ever be pinned down.

Miss Naude had a boyfriend. She only saw him once a week; we knew because every Thursday, she would dress up. Make-up, earrings, hair combed sleekly to one side, high heels and perfume. She even changed her handbag on a Thursday. She was different as well, happy. She didn't slump in her chair as she did on other days or frown or sigh sadly at the end of every lesson as if she had just taught us some terrible truth about life.

There was Mrs Thomas, too, who had long dark hair down to her waist and who never wore it up, so she looked like a 1970s Cher. Her husband, she told us, wouldn't allow her to cut it and said that if she did, he would leave her. We saw her hair as a testament of her love for him. We subscribed to an idea of womanhood and what we thought men wanted us to be. At the same time, we thought we'd never be any of these women, even Miss Ndlovu. Life had other things planned for us and staying in a dusty one-horse town in Africa was not one of them.

In that last term of our school lives, in particular, as the gently expanding warmth of September stretched into the hazy scorch of October and finally into the rains of November, when our final exams hung over us like a jailer swinging his bunch of keys in the faces of desperate convicts, all we could think about was leaving. Our final concerts, plays, tennis matches and even the exams themselves took on the air of something coming to an end, something to be treasured, but not pined for; something we had outgrown.

It was only recently when I returned to Bulawayo shortly after my divorce from David, a single mother and busy with the demands of balancing work and home life, that I understood some of the decisions that Miss Parker had taken. I saw her not so long ago; it was just after I saw Mrs Thomas, now known by her maiden name of Royston and sporting a blonde bob and a fake dark brown tan that only served to highlight the lines on her slightly sagging face. Miss Parker, however, seemed not to have aged at all. She was wearing navy blue trousers and a long-sleeved white shirt and there upon her head was a little white sailor's hat. Somewhere, somehow, she had learnt a lesson, and whether she was right or wrong about it, is not for me to decide. Although the path she chose to follow may not be for everywoman I couldn't help thinking, as she crossed the street, that she cut a figure of quiet dignity as her little tugboat pulled into harbour.

POETRY IS...

Ignatius T. Mabasa

Poetry is a white child
Lost in the darkness of a cinema house
Holding my black hand
Calling me daddy....

NOT SLAVES TO FASHION

Mzana Mthimkhulu

The meeting to make arrangements for Jabulani's wedding was going on smoothly until Thobekile raised the question of catering.

"Are family members going to do the catering or are we hiring one of the women's clubs to do it?" A secretary's notepad rested on her jean-clad thighs. She flicked back her dreadlocks as her eyes swept round the eleven attendants in the sitting-room. Her gaze finally rested on the chairperson, Uncle Zwana. Like Thobekile, most of those present were in their thirties.

"What women's club?" Zwana asked, turning his bald head to look at the meeting's secretary. He sat on a high chair and looked down at everyone else over his heavy-rimmed spectacles. At fifty-eight he was the second oldest person in the room. The oldest being his sixty-year old brother sekaDumisani, who had come all the way from the rural home for the meeting. The two sat next to each other.

"Don't talk in riddles, Thobekile," Uncle Zwana continued. "What is this women's club?"

"Move with the times, Uncle," Thobekile laughed. "There are now women's clubs who, for a fee, do all the cooking, serving and washing up at family gatherings."

Uncle Zwana emitted a sarcastic chuckle. "Here is a pig getting fat before nine eyes!" He clapped his hands once and slowly shook his head to show his amazement.

"Come on, Thobekile, you mean you are actually suggesting that we hire such a crowd for our family function?" His voice boomed with a mixture of disgust and shock.

85

"Why not?" nakaBongani demanded, stretching out her long neck and looking her uncle in the eye. "It's now the fashionable thing to do. For instance, at the last wedding I attended..."

"It was not a Masuku wedding," Zwana cut in with a dismissive wave of the hand. "We the Masukus have never been and will never be slaves to fashion." He had moved to the edge of the chair, and wildly gesticulated to emphasize his words.

"Just because some spineless families are doing away with tradition does not mean that we too have to jump on the bandwagon. Look back into our history and you will discover that we have always been a proud and resourceful family. We do not allow strangers to invade our kitchens and cook for us. And then – as if this were not enough of a disgrace – serve us in our own homes, at our own functions. My brother would turn in his grave if I allowed such a practice to rear its ugly head at his son's wedding. Surely every member of the Masuku family in here knows this?"

Zwana's piercing eyes slowly went round the room daring anyone to disagree.

SekaDumisani cleared his throat. "You are right, son of my father. What right thinking person can disagree with the plain truth?" he asked, spreading out his hands. "Cooking and serving is a family affair, end of story."

Zwana smiled and nodded to acknowledge the words of wisdom from his elder brother. Still smiling, he turned to his niece, "So in answer to your question, Thobekile, we are not hiring some crew of third rate cooks and waitresses calling themselves a catering club to come and crowd us at our family gathering. We will serve ourselves as we have always done through the ages. We have our own daughters and daughters-in-law who enjoy cooking and serving the family. Everyone knows that food tastes best if it is cooked and served by your own people, not hired hands.

"Now let us have volunteers for the catering sub-committee. I nominate maDube to head the sub-committee. She has done it well in the past and I am sure she will continue to excel. Not surprising really, we the Masukus have always chosen our wives well." He chuckled at his joke before continuing. "Anyway, any more volunteers for the rest of the sub-committee?"

MaDube broke the brief silence that followed. "I think we ought to discuss the catering question further before setting up a catering committee."

As a daughter-in-law in the family, maDube did not have the confidence and authority her thirty-six years suggested. Her voice quivered and she nervously looked round appealing for support.

"Come on, maDube," Zwana drawled, "you want the meeting to be bogged down on one small issue? We have already agreed that we do it in the time-tested method. Anyway, what new facts can you bring to the subject?"

"Go on, maDube", nakaBongani smiled encouragingly at her sister-in-law. "In this meeting, even daughters-in-law are allowed to speak their minds. After all, Uncle Zwana is not your direct father-in-law. So you don't need to observe the tradition of respect. Speak out girl." There was scattered laughter as attention turned to maDube.

Before maDube could speak, the hostess, Jabulani's mother, opened the door from the kitchen and walked in. An aroma of freshly baked scones wafted into the room. She carried a plastic jug of water and a small bowl. Her first stop was at sekaDumisani. She respectfully knelt before him and lifted the jug to pour out the water for him to wash his hands. SekaDumisani scowled. He disapproved of doing away with the custom of washing hands directly in the bowl. For him, all washing with the same water symbolized unity of the family. He was, however, consoled by observance of the custom that the oldest was the first to be served.

As requested by the hostess and her aunt, Thobekile went to the kitchen to fetch the scones. Soon everyone had washed their hands and was picking up scones from a plate on the coffee table.

"Excellent illustration of the fruits of doing it yourself." Uncle Zwana nodded as he munched his third scone. "Well baked at home, well served. Transport is the next item on the agenda."

"I think maDube still has something to say on catering," nakaBongani said.

Again, everyone looked at maDube. "Well I definitely think we must hire a catering club." This time maDube's voice was steady and clear. She sat upright and had the confidence of a well-prepared lawyer. "My father-in-law here talks about a proud family tradition of serving ourselves, but what has that meant for some of us? During the twelve years I have been married into his family, I have attended five weddings but I have not enjoyed a single one of them. How could I when I was expected to cook under the most difficult conditions, serve a multitude of revellers, wash up a mountain of plates and pots and at the end of it all, clean up a place that looked like it had been hit by a cyclone? I have been a busy bee before, during and after the weddings."

"*Nkosi yami!*" Uncle Zwana exclaimed in mock admiration. "So you have single-handedly done all that work? I didn't know that we had Superwoman in the family!" Now serious, he continued, "Look, I think you exaggerate a

87

bit here and there, but you have made your point. Let's now move on to…"

"I haven't finished," maDube interrupted. "I want the meeting to appreciate that, at the past family weddings, I have never had a chance to sing along with others, dance, meet people, admire the bridal party, feast and so on. For me all the weddings have just been glorified hard labour. I would really love to dress up for a family wedding, put on some make-up, and afterwards appear in the photographs and videos. In other words, I would love to enjoy myself at a family wedding. But without a hired catering club, my fate is that of sweating it out at the open fires, washing up and cleaning."

"Don't monopolise the floor, maDube", Zwana warned, wagging a threatening finger. "Remember, at your wedding you did not do any work. You were a pampered princess throughout the day and well into the night. Family members were there to sweat it out and make the day the most enjoyable and memorable one you have ever had. Now you scoff at returning the favour at your brother-in-law's wedding. That's gratitude for you!" He nudged his elder brother who nodded in agreement.

MaDube sighed before speaking. "Firstly, I did not enjoy myself at my wedding. I was too tense and anxious. Throughout the day, I was in mortal fear that something would go terribly wrong. Secondly, after working flat out at five weddings, I think I have paid my dues. Check all the pictures and videos of the family weddings I have attended – I am not there. Who is interested in a mere cook? No, it is time I joined the fun. We must hire a catering club," she concluded with emphasis.

The women murmured their support and beamed sympathetic smiles at her. Zwana only half heard what maDube was saying. To his delight, he realised that all of the people who had indicated their support for hiring a catering club were women. There were a total of five women in a meeting of twelve.

"We have heard both sides of this catering issue," Zwana summed up in a business-like manner. "Now let us put it to a vote and move on to the next item. Hands up all those who want us to spend our hard earned money on some women's club."

Ten hands went up. Only Zwana and sekaDumisani did not lift up their hands.

Zwana blinked in disbelief and his jaw dropped. Just what was happening to the Masuku family? How could such a foreign and stupid idea muster so much support? More painful, how could most Masuku men go along with such heresy? He tried to establish eye contact with the men, but they avoided his gaze. Could this be just a bad joke, he wondered? It had to be.

"*Madoda,*" he appealed to the men, "perhaps you misunderstood the vote. It is only those who want us to throw away our culture, our proud traditions, our very being, who are supposed to put up their hands now. For us who know where we are coming from and where we are going, our turn to lift up our hands is yet to come."

The ten hands remained up.

"There is no need for any further voting," a delighted Thobekile said. "The majority is agreed that we hire a club. I will get three quotations from which we can select the right club." Thobekile stopped talking and looked up at her uncle to signal that he proceed with the meeting. The chairperson stared straight ahead with a blank expression on his face. Not a word came out of his mouth.

"Come on, Uncle Zwana," Thobekile urged. "We must not be bogged down on one small issue. Let us move on to the next item on the agenda, which is transport. How many private cars will be available on the big day?" Three people pledged their cars and some said they would be approaching friends who had cars.

The hostess had now joined the meeting. "Jabu phoned this morning," she said. "He advised that four of his workmates and friends in Johannesburg have pledged to provide their cars on the wedding day."

Zwana dragged his thoughts away from his turmoil and confusion. He tried with limited success to follow the discussion on transport. As for sekaDumisani, he could not wait to get back to his rural home where his word was law.

THE PENCIL TEST

Diana Charsley

"So you spring cleaning today?" Darlene, hands on hips, gazed at bare clothes rails reflecting weak candlelight. Dawn, to whom she addressed the question, stared at the floor, with her arms wrapped tightly across her chest. The shop staff, each whispering sorry, sorry, disappeared into the cold dark.

Although she had been expecting it, nothing could have prepared her for what happened. They were heard before they were seen: a roaring entourage of navy blue *Defenders*, followed by a seven-tonne truck and an assortment of gleaming late model sedans and SUVs. Screaming to a halt, their doors opened simultaneously disgorging all occupants. With the price-control task force leading, the entire party entered Larger Than Life, Dawn's exclusive shop for generously proportioned women. Shouting at Dawn and accusing her of treason, the policemen tore though her files for evidence of economic sabotage while the policewomen confiscated the best dresses for exhibits. Shoving Dawn in front of them they instructed the trembling saleswomen to mark down all prices by sixty per cent as they went past. Then Dawn – along with Mrs Ncube from Afro-styles Hair Salon, Mrs Sibanda the local café owner and Mr Vithal from the bakery – was thrust into the seven-tonner. A collection of offending items and baton-armed cadres completed the load. Well-elevated Dawn witnessed the task-force groupies' shopping orgy. The customers, many regular, shopped happily apart from one or two spats over the same dress (the most ornate one split down the middle after a heavyweight tug-of-war). It reminded Dawn of Solomon settling a baby dispute. The noise of breaking glass diverted her attention and she turned to see the glass frontage of Mrs Sibanda's shop spray over the pavement. Another jostling crowd was fighting for bargain-priced *Mazoe Orange Crush*. Mrs Sibanda screamed down at them while her daughter in the shop flagged helpless arms in an attempt at crowd control. Just before setting off, Mr Chapoto from Abie's Restaurant, and a crate of over-priced *Castle*, and a couple of menus joined them: further evidence of criminal activity. Their custodians eyed the beer lovingly.

After hours of standing in the police courtyard, relieved by bursts of threatening interrogation, Dawn paid a hefty fine to avoid a night in the detention cells. By evening she was back at the shop with a power cut and Darlene cracking jokes.

"You try to turn everything into a joke don't you?" Dawn hit out.

"Honey, if you'd lived my life you would have learnt to see the funny side of things."

"Well right now I've got nothing to laugh about and life hasn't turned out so bad for you. For one thing you were born in South Africa; you can leave this place any time you want to. Not like me, I'm stuck here."

"What makes you think I want to go back there? Ever heard of the immorality act, honey? 1950? The year I was born?"

"What you getting at?" How was it that Darlene always managed to turn the conversation to herself? Dawn thought peevishly.

"In 1950 my father was busy rogering my ma in the garage when all of a sudden crash bash and there were police all over the place."

Dawn looked puzzled, "Why would the police break in on a married couple having sex?"

"Married couple?" Darlene snorted, "My ma was a house-girl and my pa a white dom-dom-dominie. They were one of the first couples to be charged under the immorality act, which made it illegal for *wit ous* to shaft kaffirs. Miss-sod-jenny they called it."

"Darlene!"

"Well it's true. My dear old dad got a suspended sentence while my ma got one year. But they let her go after six months to save the embarrassment of having me born in prison."

"Why so much longer for your mother?"

"Oh, the judge waved my ma's knickers for all to see and said she'd corrupted a good Christian man. Anyway his congregation did not think too much of that and bulldozed the offending garage to the ground. He left town I am told."

91

"So how come you ended up in Bulawayo?"

"Well, my mother's family chucked her out but, shame the poor baby, it wasn't her fault. To cut a long story short, I was adopted by a coloured couple who'd had enough of South Africa. Pop worked on the railways so Bulawayo was an obvious choice."

"I never knew," Dawn murmured, her own troubles momentarily forgotten.

Darlene poked her head into Dawn's office, "Now what's the matter with you? You getting to be a full time job, girl!"

"I can't carry on. It's just too much."

"Tell aunty all about it."

"Well you know, because I can't get anything here, I've had a runner smuggle in material for Bongi's team to make up in the back?"

"Ja."

"And you know I've only been selling to customers I can trust, like Siphiwe whose mother in England is selling my garments to all her friends who can't find anything to suit them over there?"

"Ja."

"Well this morning one of those political heavy-weights, a former customer, came in here and wanted to know why I had nothing for her. I mumbled something about the textile mills closing down and she came right up close and spat threats into my face."

"What she say?"

"First of all she said didn't I know that all shops not operating would be taken over by people who had the capacity to make them productive. Then she sneered and told me that even if I did stock up again I would have the indigenisation and empowerment bill to think about. What did she mean?"

"Oh that. Haven't you seen the paper today?"

"Never read it."

"Well you should. Know thine enemy, as they say." Darlene pulled a paper out of her voluminous bag. "It says here that the Minister of State for Indigenization and Economic Empowerment – oow – what a mouthful! No wonder they get their underlings to introduce them. Anyway, this guy says this bill is to correct all the political wrongs of the past. According to this law fifty-one percent of a business must be held by indigenous persons."

"Well I was born here, and my father, so I guess that qualifies me," said Dawn.

"Sorry china, no such luck. According to this article you are only indigenous if, before 1980, you suffered on the basis of race. Hey, check this out, that includes us coloureds. As for you, the Minister says: 'A Zimbabwean-born white cannot qualify. He has to prove that he has been disadvantaged by the colonisation.' Did you suffer?"

"Well," Dawn began.

"Ja, I'm sure you did, especially on Sunday afternoon when there were no servants to ring your little bell for."

"Ok, ok, so I was privileged, you don't have to rub it in," Dawn responded hotly. "I can't help my childhood."

"Keep your hat on, just a joke," said Darlene, hardly noticing Dawn's outburst, "that means we will have to pursue a second option."

"What on earth are you talking about?"

"Well if you didn't suffer under the colonial regime, we'll just have to make you one of the new elite."

"Another one of your jokes I suppose?"

"No, this could work. What the *dominee* did for me I can do for you – make you coloured."

"Ha, ha, ha," Dawn barked mechanically.

"Have you heard of the pencil test?"

"Oh that. Well I guess I'd fail that now, gravity's winning hands down at this stage of my life. But I'd do better than you. You could hide a whole pack of crayons under those boobs of yours and walk out of a shop with nobody noticing."

"Jealousy will get you nowhere but, Miss Piano Lessons, that is not what I am talking about. In the same year as I was born…"

"It seems like everything happened the year you were born."

"Of course. Anyway, in 1950, there was this law passed in South Africa to make sure that everyone knew their place – the population registration act. Once you know who you were you also knew where to live."

"I'm not so sheltered that I don't know about apartheid. It also happened here in case you did not notice. But what's that got to do with a pencil test? Sounds more like a Miss World selection to me."

"No the pencil was for the hair, not the boobs. You see some of us looked quite pale and some of the Afrikaners looked like us, so, if they couldn't decide what we were by colour, they put a pencil in the hair and told us to shake our heads. If it shook out you were white and if it stayed in you were coloured." Dawn shook her head. "I told you you were sheltered," added

93

Darlene.

"Thanks for the history lesson, but what's the pencil test got to do with my predicament?"

"I told you, I'm going to give you the honour of becoming one of us," said Darlene, bowing theatrically.

"But you always tell me that I look as if I've crawled out from under a rock. You can't change my genes you know."

"But we can make it look as if they've changed. With this water we are getting through our taps these days – once a week if we're lucky – all you have to do is soak around in that for an hour or so and no one could tell the difference."

"I suppose I would have to soak my head as well. How do you expect me to breathe?"

"I'll give you a straw."

"Thanks for your concern. Ok, that's the skin and I know what you'll suggest for the hair – black dye and tight perm?"

Darlene nodded at Dawn enthusiastically, "Now you're catching the drift."

"And for the eyes I'd have to wear sunglasses all the time unless I can get hold of those tinted contacts." Dawn's shoulders started to shake.

"Well I'm glad to see that you're laughing for a change, please let me in on the joke."

"I'm just imagining that woman who came in this morning finding the business under new management."

"She would be fooled just so long as you don't open that larny mouth of yours. I'm going to have to give you el-o-cu-tion lessons," said Darlene, exaggerating the working of her mouth. Dawn put out her tongue in response.

"But what about my ID card?" Dawn continued.

"What about it?" Darlene asked.

"Well I've been told that some of the numbers show what race group you belong to."

"Have you got yours on you?"

"Here," Dawn said, picking through her wallet and handing it to Darlene.

"Take a look at this. You see the last two numbers after the letter? They are 00. And look at mine – see, the same."

"Hey yours says J00, and after all this time of you telling me that your father was a Dutch-Reformed minister. You should be going to the synagogue!"

94

"Oh, so now you've taken on my job of being the joker. What about yours it says ZOO, so much for all your fine breeding."

"We also share the first two numbers, 08. We must really be joined at the hip," Dawn noted.

"That's for Bulawayo. So much information on such a small disc. My mother would have had to carry round a 96-page book at all times."

At home Dawn could not sleep. Her mood swung between despair and ironic hope. She debated the drastic measures needed to save her business – would it work? How would her friends and family react? Dawn, the ultra-conservative. But she had been changing since her friendship with Darlene, Darlene who always challenged her with her mocking humour. Why not? Dawn thought – it's not as if the transformation would be permanent? She would show Darlene she had balls as Darlene crudely put it. And the family? Well they would just have to see her in a different light.

Giving up on sleep she decided to bath. The tightly rationed water had come on during the night and was now running clean. She filled a shallow bath, and then filled it some more. Opening the medicine cabinet above the basin she noticed a bottle of potassium permanganate and remembered her son, Alan, playing the part of an Indian in a school play. They had submerged him in a bath-full of permanganate. The effect was startling: his blue eyes contrasted starkly with the nut-brown skin. Dawn impulsively grabbed the bottle and emptied it into the bath. The dye swirled in lazy curls; Dawn stretched the patterns out with her foot. Lifting it out of the water she noticed an instant tan, something that had eluded her all her life. "Why not?" she said, quickly immersing herself before she could change her mind. Unsure of the dye's properties she got out quickly and, as she dried herself, she stared at her reflection, fascinated with her new image. No doubt Darlene would bring her down to earth by comparing her with a pecan nut but Dawn did not care. She felt as if she had thrown off her mousey self and could now stand up to anybody. Even 'that woman'.

At the shop in the morning she heard stifled giggles from the sewing room. Well if I can make them laugh in times like this, good, she smiled as she phoned for an appointment with the hairdresser.

"Whoa!" yelled Darlene as she came through the door. She made an exaggerated exit and put on her sunglasses to peer at the shop sign. "I see this shop is still called Larger Than Life. Is it under new management?"

"In a manner of speaking, yes" said Dawn, pulling down the corners of her mouth to suppress a smile.

"Well this time you leapt before you looked," Darlene said with her eyebrows pulled into her hairline, "I came to tell you that you didn't need to do anything because the legislation does not apply to family businesses. What did you do to your skin?"

"My secret."

"Well you certainly are a dark one, excuse the pun; I would never have thought it of you. So what are you going to do now, bath in *Jik*?"

"No, I'm off to the hairdresser to finish the effect."

"You're serious aren't you?" Darlene was intrigued.

"Actually I've decided to lighten up. I've been thinking about what you said yesterday, about how having it tough made you see the funny side of things. Things are going to get a lot tougher, so I'm taking a leaf out of your book."

"Right on, girl."

"And I can't wait for 'that woman' to come back. How about those elocution lessons you promised?"

PLEASURE

Chaltone Tshabangu

Pleasure. I say pleasure because he said woman and it disturbs me to know that he thinks this way. *Yet*, there is this small voice in me that keeps on saying *yet*, it infuriates me. Pleasure. Pleasure? No. His choice word was 'woman' where he could have said 'pleasure' and 'pleasure' where he could have said 'woman'. Each time he spoke that way, the image of Mother superimposed itself upon everything and unsettled me.

How do I know what he could have said? I know what he is like when he is speaking as what he terms a 'real man'.

"Pleasure," he told his friends that Sunday morning, "is a wily fox to be hunted down with baying hounds, foaming horses, cocked rifles and cat-calls and curses and *wooo-wii,*" he cried, "the blood-thirsty violence of lust!" I thought that the idea of English lords and fox hunting was rather off but the words he used, the words he whispered in our own language carried a disquieting potency and were, true to form, charged with an eroticism that made one of his friends hastily reach for the mug of millet beer at their feet and the other to cross his legs and laugh an uncertain little laugh.

"You will find pleasure secreted in the folds of her skin, in her voice, pleasure like truffles to be mined from the pores of her skin. It is something in her that is always breathless for a strange sort of freedom. Yet with a woman, you may not experience pleasure at all until you blow away the dust of morals, mop off the sweat imposed by society and eat like a man, for she is food. A woman is food. So, in setting pleasure free, you free yourself too, eh, boy, do you not?" Here he slapped my back as I bent down to place a plateful of steaming, braaied tripe and casings at their feet. I think I laughed

97

but held my words for I knew my place. "*Yasseright*, boy!" One of his friends crowed, but the other frowned and his displeasure was noted. "Ah, but the boy must be a man and the only way for him to learn to be a man is *my* way. I wouldn't want him to be like those... those... pansies with pierced ears and nose jobs and ancestors know what else! No. Must make a man of him myself, the way my father made of me, eh, boy?" As if my name was Boy.

"Set her free. Like a bird. Like a bird," he repeated, as if one of us had meant to contradict him. "A woman is like those stupid sparrows that fly into your house and cannot find their way out. They keep slamming against the window panes, confounded by...," here he paused, absently tugging at his earlobe, "let us say confounded by the philosophy of a window pane," he breathed the words out, English words. His friend, the one who is a teacher, burst out laughing. Oh, my father is a great one for ruffling an intellectual feather or two when the occasion suits him.

"So you catch the poor bird, feel its poor little heart slamming against its thin rib-cage and don't you feel sorry for the poor, stupid thing? So, you set it down on the ground and wait for it to fly away. It doesn't, not for a while anyway, which is time enough for you to bring down your booted foot and crash its stupid head. That is how to keep a woman in hand." They laughed, uproariously. He was drunk, of course.

I fear what I may do.

He introduced me to the blank spaces of a *Madison Toasted* cigarette packet; space enough to be personal without being sentimental and to be sentimental without being unmanly. "Keys in my left shoe," written in his choppy, upright handwriting between the bit that lists the life-giving ingredients of cigarette smoke: yum-yum carbon monoxide, nectar of cyanide, invigorating nicotine and delicious tar, and the words in blue which tell you in lofty superlatives how *Madison Toasted* cigarettes are made for your pleasure.

"Grease under the bread bin," he sometimes writes, grease being his slang for money. I collect empty *Madison Toasted* cigarette packets the way some men net butterflies for trophies. In our room, the blank surface of a cigarette packet is the refrigerator door in some people's houses; therein beats the pulse of their lives.

Last year, on my fourteenth birthday – not that we celebrate birthdays in our home – I wrote about lung cancer, thanks to my biology teacher. I squeezed in all the text beneath the packet's declaration, 'Premium Quality'. For six months afterwards there was no cigarette smoke in our room until one

Friday when Mother came in from the rurals, unannounced. She got a blue eye for her oversight. I got mine too, for what he termed "unmanly solidarity with a woman." The following morning, after he had left for work – his short hair, dyed jet black, neatly combed and parted on the left, his starched trousers that Mother pressed until they could stand all on their own, deftly folded at the flared bottoms and clipped with wooden washing pegs so as not to collect grease from his oiled and polished ten speed *Humber*. He looked cool and disgustingly dapper. Women would as usual pause in their sweeping-the-yard-and-road chore to drop a curtsey and call out a greeting while his *Humber*'s machinery went tika-tika-tika under him – Mother waited until she was certain he was gone, then applied a hot compress to my swollen eye and remarked rather pithily, "The tale is told that it is no bravery to wipe your bottom with prickly pears." We were attacked by the giggles for quite a long time. It took me longer, however, to differentiate between tears and tears of laughter.

The ancient *Spring Master* bed, raised on four, empty two litre *Dulux* paint tins takes up most of the room we rent. I sleep on the floor. Mother comes in once a fortnight to do our laundry and, as she is fond of saying, to cook us a decent meal. Then I sleep with the landlord's twins, Allan and Ellen, head-to-toe fashion on the kitchen floor. Once Mother's laundry has been taken down from the clothes-line, pressed and neatly folded or hung from nails on the wall, she goes back to our rural home.

Twice a week, regular as clockwork, I sleep directly under the old *Spring Master*. I used to plug my ears with cotton wool kindly donated by Ellen. I watch the regular movements of the coiled springs, the rhythmic squeaks mingling with the barely suppressed groans and snarls coming from above the mattress. Mostly I am too sloshed to care, too sloshed to be bothered by the disturbing stirrings of my own loins as I lie under the bed.

"It's a man thing, son," he wrote between 'Danger: Smoking is Harmful to Health' and '*Madison*' on an empty cigarette packet. "One day you will understand these things." I fear what I may understand. I did not reply. We never reply. There is no need to. Our lives are explanation enough.

The sight of a neighbour's pair of white sheets billowing in the sun, in the wind and the imagined spray of a million tiny globules of combined bleach – *Jik* – and *Stay Soft* fabric softener lower my hunched shoulders and I find that I can inhale and relax. I inhale and find it within me to think of Mother as a tall and proud African woman, not one stooped by rural labour, not one who has to wash sheets soiled by strange women. I look at sheets as they snap and crack in a rogue wind and find that I have the power within myself to drink some more, for nothing is to be willingly understood.

The last time I tried talking to Mother, she said, "Child, it is foolish to prescribe a pot-full of boiled beans to a case of acute flatulence." The way she hugs pain close to herself, as if to comfort pain, as if she does not know that even pain huggles close, it saddens me. You are a man, the look in her eyes says, you will understand these things one day. No, I will not feel sorry, not for my mother.

"The problem," Ellen whispers, snuggling close, "is us."

"Us?"

"Ssh! Yes, us. Women. The love for the close prison of matrimonial bliss is irresistible."

"Liar." It's my mother we are talking about.

"She gives you 'Thou shalt nots', does she not?"

"Shuttup, Ellen." But the little voice inside me tells me that Ellen is correct, whether I will admit the truth or not. Trouble began with the very first Thou Shalt Not. God was uncompromising. Mother is the same. But then, so is Father. Thorns and thistles and pain and sweat were a result of the first Thou Shalt Not and complete lack of compromise.

I close my eyes and pray for a rainbow, but the image I get is of a woman standing by a cold hearth, in one hand she holds a pan of cold ashes and her other hand reaches out as if for the sky. Each pore of her black, black skin is a tiny mouth twisted into a maw of private anguish. Mother. Oh Mother! She knows that I know she knows, yet, she gently cuffs my head and states the obvious, "That man is your father, remember that". So I sip a little wine, privately. Not that he would stop me – drinking alcohol is part of manliness – but because I know that I am too young and there is school and God, too. But it's only a little cheap wine, guardian angel, to keep insanity at bay. I drink just a little, remembering Nebuchadnezzar who challenged God and had grass for lunch for three years. Also, it gives me the strength to wonder about Mother's God, who makes her so willing to welcome sorrow. I gulp down glass after glass of liquid fire so I can lie still under the bed, even though the Torquemada inside won't let me rest. I fear what I may do.

Beneath the cheerful words 'smoking can cause death' I wrote my first answer-demanding question, "Why?" They had fought the previous night and Mother took the beating in her usual way; complete silence. He did not reply, of course. Neither did God.

Friday nights. We wait for the drunken Allan to snore before Ellen turns around and places her lips on mine. Together, afterwards, we listen to the sounds coming from our room and she whispers, "Swinish, *este?*" I hardly know what *este* means and, I am sure, neither does she, but it is one of those words she has heard somewhere and liked. It's mildly annoying, actually, the way she keeps on using the word.

"Swinish, *este?*"

"Thoroughly," I reply, a part of me throbbing pleasurably in the grip of her greedy hand.

These days, there is something not really nice about the way Ellen doesn't show concern, even for herself. I hurt her, deliberately, a little at first with words that always want to come out strong and vindictive, then physically. She takes it all in her stride. Her little cries point at pleasure, not pain.

It was not long before I found an empty cigarette packet on the bed and, on the side where '20' and *'Madison'* are printed was written, "Only a fool will marry the girl next door". Of course, I told myself, nice and apt Devil's truth. But after that, I began to look at Ellen again, in a different light.

"I'm thinking of leaving," I told Ellen the morning one of those fat, devil-nay-care strangers with a smoker's blackened heels left my parents' bed. She did not reply.

Mother came that same day. Mother was happy. She hummed as she changed the sheets. She sang as she washed the soiled sheets the following day. In the afternoon she called me to the washing line to perform a ritual we have held for as long as I could remember.

She took the clean sheet down, folded it lengthwise twice and gave me one side while she took the other. Heels dug in, we tugged, stretched and pulled, meanwhile holding in breath and fighting down the urge to break down and laugh. We always ended up dissolving with the giggles anyway. I hardly know why. The second bed sheet was the most difficult to do because by then we had been weakened by the laughter. There were times when one of us would be hauled in, leading to a fall. She would re-wash the soiled sheet again, and again we would engage in the ritual once it dried. Neighbours opened their windows and stared, shook their heads and pulled their windows shut once more, knowing smiles on their faces.

Last night they had one of those silent rows and he beat her up, quietly

101

because the landlord said no noise in my house, please. I smelt spilt *Jik* and blood and something else that came from within myself. But I bit it down until the morning. She would not let me wipe away the blood; she would not let me do a thing.

"Mother, why?" But she did not reply. She just lay on the floor, next to the old *Spring Master*. I know that I have always had something inside me, something dark and mean, something always spoiling for a fight. It came out then, burning for a slice of light.

"I try to tell you, Mother, but you, you don't care." My voice was playing nasty tricks on me, cracking and rising in volume until it was something big and uncontrollable. My vision was blurring. "I tell you everyday that he is a bastard who will kill you with AIDS one day –" I never finished the sentence. She leapt up onto her feet, rolled up the sleeves of her blouse and punched me in the mouth. When I tried to speak she punched my mouth again. Slowly I slid down to the floor and the most unmanly thing happened, I couldn't hold back the tears.

"Never," she panted, eyes flashing. "Don't you ever speak about your father like that again!"

Ellen followed me down the road. It was still dark and, strangely enough, quiet for a high density suburb street.

"Don't go," she pleaded, "you don't have to go." I looked at Ellen for quite a while and realized that in a few years, despite all her bluster and bravado, she would be like my mother. She too was destined to stand behind high fences, an apologetic grin on her face, waiting to be acknowledged. She too would lie down on her man's urine-bathed floor, spread-eagled, and wait to be needed. She will always be hungry for a sign of approbation, even a smile, as if a man lives on woman alone. Such women must be selfish, I thought as I turned and walked away. Such spinelessness and such hunger can only come out of selfishness, even guilt. Born guilty, the way Mother's God wants her to be. But Mother, what was she really guilty of?

"Please," Ellen whined behind me and I stopped. I could hit her, snap her head back with a back-hander and punch her in the guts. However, I only had the strength to walk away. I walked away.

And the Rains Came

Pathisa Nyathi

Once they said
it was a place of slaughter,
not of cattle
or goats, or sheep,
no, of human beings.
Bulawayo is dying indeed.

Boreholes dotted all over the city,
a sprawling rural metropolis of a rare kind.
Beyond dusk and into the inviting night
women and children
delicately balance water containers
on their heads of permed hair.

Pushcarts, in varying degrees of disrepair,
wobble and bob precariously along
the scarred and potholed streets
on their way to the boreholes.
Bullyboys drive the fairer sex away,
first come first served ignored,
and get the water to sell.

"*Amanzi*, $20 000 only!"
It's money for the scuds,
traditional brew in Iraqi missile containers,
unemployed youths finding easy money.
Vulnerable children
resort to water sources unorthodox,
final resting places
of disease-causing bacteria from errant effluent.

Twice a week taps squirt municipal water,
conservation through water shedding, they call it,
now a dry mark of a dying city.
A dark ominous ZINWA cloud hovers above

like vultures at a good kill.
Bulawayo, the place of slaughter!

Bowsers, small and big,
zoom up and down
taking water to high places
shunned by the lazy pipes.
Tense scrambles ensue
of fighting buckets on the leash.
Long winding queues angrily form
of drawn scowling faces,
with their weary feet
screeching their containers towards an emptying bowser.

Nonchalant babies strapped on backs,
mothers slog and trudge along the dusty streets
to the waiting darkness of their houses –
electricity these days is more off than on.
Another depressing trip to the prowling bush
to get a cord of skimpy firewood
to be delicately balanced on the same weary head.
Bulawayo, the place of slaughter!

Small children scamper and strut about in the street,
oblivious to the gathering clouds in the sky.
The enchanting smell of fresh rain
wafts through the enduring odours
from loose rank sewage from toilets and factories.
Swarms of swallows drift ahead in flights of bliss and rapture
and grand expectations.

Frolicking children gaze at
the heavens and see the swallows
beckoning the obliging clouds,
"Come rain, rain come
come, so we may eat *amakhomane*!"
The effluent and its pungent smell
are set to go,
at long last, Bulawayo shall live again.

RAIN IN JULY

Fungai Rufaro Machirori

Curdled. I learnt that word in my mother's kitchen, peering into a bowl in which she mixed ingredients for a Victoria Sandwich. As she stirred beaten eggs into the pale fluff of creamed butter and sugar, the silky swirl began to separate into a gory mess like vomit. Curdled. That's how she described it – the eggs' coldness shocking the butter into fickle specks floating through the mixture. Curdled, like my blood against the flow of what was once warm.

I always escape to the easiest places when overwhelmed by the brutality of the present. The night my father died, I retreated into memories of his battered brown suede moccasins. I remembered their worn rubber soles and the moist sweaty smell from inside their felt lining with the fading logo that read Champion. Every evening when he came home, he ranged those size 11s next to my size 2 black glass shoes and Mama's sandals and then, barefoot, he swooped me up into the air and spun me into giggles, clasping my chest tight with his wide palms.

My Champion was gone.

And now I saw my mother's kitchen wedge the gap between the halves of who I'd been and who I was going to be. I saw the Sunday sunlight slash through the flimsy lace curtain onto my mother's hands, felt the oven's warmth waft through the room and smelt the sweetness of vanilla essence from its half-opened bottle. I wanted to stay there – ambiguous and safe – not having to proceed to the second half of me where I stood looking into Sipho's eyes, our fingertips punctured and the nauseating smell of methylated spirits seeping bitterly onto our tongues.

Why didn't I remember something about Sipho and I? Why Mama? Why didn't I hide in the memories of the first time we met, or kissed, or said, "I love you" to each other? If I called on remembrance, the images would come cascading through my mind. But maybe I didn't want them to. Maybe I wanted to forget that slow Saturday when we first met and it all began.

Sipho's best friend, Eddy, was my roommate's boyfriend. Mary and I shared a cramped room in one of the halls of residence on campus. She was studying political science and Eddy was a fourth year student in her department, one semester shy of his degree. We were just one semester in, but Mary had already settled in to an effortless routine of late night orgies of alcohol and political protest. She and Eddy tried to coax me to join them, but I always had an excuse not to – laundry that needed doing, or the impossible task of tidying our tiny space overrun with books, clothes and cutlery.

Mary thought I was boring – and bored. But I assured her that I had enough to keep me busy with my chores and biochemistry textbooks. The weekends gave me time to catch up and, that Saturday, I had found a copy of a science research article that I had been eager to read over a lazy weekend. But Mary and Eddy begged me to put that off for a while and go out with them. That was the first time I met Sipho – one hand stretched over the steering wheel, leaning back into the driver's seat of his rickety, scraped, dusty *Pulsar*, yelling loudly to us to get in quickly.

Red Eagles United had just scored a goal to level the match against premiership title chasers Allstars F.C. The radio commentator bellowed the details as we bundled into the car, Sipho and Eddy excitedly exchanging celebratory handshakes. I sat in the back with Mary, digging my knees into the bony back of Eddy's seat listening to the three of them swell with glee at the prospect of earning a valuable point in the fight against relegation.

Soon the commentary mellowed and our ride squealed and shuddered through town to the fringes of Balfour, a suburb of endless rows of broken, hollow, grim apartment buildings, where children – brown, pink, yellow, big, small – hurled plastic balls into clouds of dust around themselves, or heckled the overweight and disabled who laboured past their games.

Sipho parked the car in front of a sad three-storey block of blue flats with curtainless broken windows. Its walls were smudged with greasy handprints and the paint was peeling away to reveal cold grey cement. We all got out of the car and walked across the pavement into the dark hallway. Sipho led us to the first wooden door on the right before inviting us into a sunless musty room, bare except for a dirty two-seat sofa in the middle.

"What makes you cry?" he asked, searching my face for my elusive eyes.

Eddy and Mary had taken their flirting to the next room and cranked up the volume of the reggae they were not listening to beyond the closed door. I felt the beat pulse through the threadbare sofa cushion as I gripped it harder, uncomfortable with the question, yet compelled by the sincerity it seemed to beg.

"The fact that my mother lost the only man she had ever loved so soon."

Those were the first words I had spoken since Eddy and Mary left. And they came out of some profound and painful place I did not often visit. I told him about my father – his smile, his smell – and those moccasins he'd used to brake in panic as his car's front tyre burst, causing him to veer uncontrollably out of our lives.

That was the first time we met. And every time afterwards there was this same continuous surge of energy, transformed into new experiences and emotions. Three and a half years swept by and I had completed my degree. I was working in a medical laboratory downtown, while Sipho owned a small but successful computer repairs workshop. The timing couldn't have been more perfect for us to get married. When I first told him I wouldn't sleep with him until he was my husband, he thought I was teasing, or that I would eventually succumb to his unrelenting offers. But each time I refused him beyond a long, passion-filled kiss, his unbelief burned into more frustration, which crackled and raged, but finally died down into respect.

I was a virgin. I had nothing to worry about in going for an HIV test. It was just a procedure, a rite of passage I believed all couples went through before marrying. Sipho had told me he had slept with girls before, but I didn't give the consequences of their nameless faces much thought as we sat in silence awaiting our results.

A man with careful eyes had plunged what looked like a staple remover quickly and painlessly into the tip of my index finger to release a surge of blood he stored in a small plastic container. Afterwards, he gave me a cotton-wool ball soaked in methylated spirits to press against the bleeding spot and told me to wait twenty minutes for the results. I sat back next to Sipho, paging through the mound of magazines on the centre table before us.

The reception room had a silence of uncertainty and expectation. I looked across from my seat to a dark-skinned man with a hollow frame and sad eyes bulging from their sunken sockets. I had diagnosed him already. He must have done the same every day he looked into the mirror, knowing what was wasting his flesh away, but running from the three letters of its name. Twenty minutes later, I felt like I was running too.

'What will you do if you find out you are positive?' The HIV counsellor's grim question returned. No one ever asked me what I would do if *Sipho* was positive. He stood before me, searching my face once more for my elusive eyes. Then a stream, something so queer, like rain in July, filled his left eye and began to course down his cheek. For a second, I believed I could catch it before it dropped to his blue cotton shirt. But I didn't try.

I thought of holding him, crying, mourning. But I didn't try. Instead, I ran to my mother's kitchen down the hallways of my mind, and stood there watching her dip the green bowl of the mess of eggs and butter into the sink she'd filled with hot water. Soon the batter warmed into a smooth ivory flow once more – the flow that Sipho and I could never enjoy. For his blood would taint my own, its cold virus making it curdle and separate.

RUM AND STILL WATERS

Lloyd Robson

I'm sat in Moe's Bar on the corner of South Portland and Lafayette. I am in pain. A lower molar has cleaved itself, and the gum holding it is infected and swollen. Eating hurts. Drinking helps, I tell myself. I am on my fourth beer. I've already had a bottle of wine. I drink Kelso – a Brooklyn beer – and dark rum chasers. I am in pain, all Mitchum-like. I attempt a cure, all Mitchum-like. My trilby hat sits on the bar, like the man himself left it there.

I got married two days ago, here in Brooklyn, at the Municipal Hall. All brass fittings and writing on the glass. Fade to black and white and it becomes a setting for a noir thriller. The hat seemed fitting. So many tests and attitudes passed that night. We woke free from having to prove anything. We are loved, it's official. We have the seal of the city, the piece of paper, the photographs, to prove it. And I'm healed, all Mitchum-like. I didn't even run. I didn't even have a hangover.

I sit in Moe's with my wedding band awkward yet right on my finger. My mouth feeling pain, a beer on the bar, my hat next to it, another rum on the way. I read as the guy next to me taps his fingers on the wood and rattles the ice in his glass in time to the South American sounds on the system. I am in pain, and I am healed. I sit drinking beer and avoiding pain and feeling the heal and reading the writings of Bulawayo; of Thabisani and Mzana and Pentecost and Dube and Tinashe and Judy and Boyce and John and Mlalazi and Diana and Julius and Pathisa; I read stories of war and fathers. I read and drink and feel pain and the heal and my hat sat on the bar, all Mitchum-like.

I sit and read and listen to the stories around me. Of the strong winter storm of the day; of snow and sleet and biting winds coming in off the

Atlantic, told by accents of Brooklyn and America and Europe and and and I read of sun and drought and no electric and no water and love and family and country and prices changing as fast and as frequent as the smoke around the pots.

I remember Bulawayo. Good people squeezed. Stores with empty shelves. One, proudly displaying overpriced tins of plum halves in syrup. Another, stacked with toilet paper, but nothing else.

I remember sitting in a bar, opposite the National Gallery – the Exchange, drinking *Castle* – 'Africa's Finest' – and writing and asking about the shop full of toilet paper. The barman shrugged. Cheaper to wipe your ass on a bank note. But not cleaner.

The Exchange: a living museum in its own right, and a history unto itself. The tile motif of the pressed metal ceiling more reminiscent of an Elizabethan noble's home than a drinking hole in Bulawayo. Only one of four ceiling fans turning. The walls stained with the colouration from exhalation, despite a lack of cigarette ends on the floor – supplies limited, singles sold by boys on street corners, sat under the lattice ironwork of colonial buildings. A stained music licence taped to the wall. Soulless mounted skulls, staring resigned and stupefied by the superficial calm of it all. Their antlers, some as big as four foot long. I asked the barman what animals they were. He didn't know.

The dark wood bar and mirrored dresser. Shelves bare but for paper banners and a smattering of empty spirit bottles. Back to the walls: ageing, rust-free advertisements; a legend of British army insignia, framed but not glassed; photographs of white, moustachioed settlers in mud-hut villages and the opening of a railway, the first engine decked in a banner proclaiming, 'Advance Rhodesia'. The *Imperial*-brand refrigerator, its cable bare and hanging from the socket, and the beer well chilled. The till without a plug and without a socket. The barman counting money, slamming shut the till drawer after each transaction, flipping down the padlock but not bothering to lock it. Many notes, little value. Young men in European football shirts playing pool in the back room. The TV flickering between football and cricket, showing games and tests from around the world. Watching Cardiff City draw with Preston, live from Ninian Park – only two or three miles from my Welsh home, viewed from the other side of many border posts and customs officials.

The drinkers, their words open yet carefully chosen. Men in suits, or T-shirts emblazoned with 'Africa Dream Safaris', sit and drink at the bar. Men in overalls sit and drink at chipped tables, on ripped-cushion benches. The arrangement is not a reflection of class or status, merely chance. They sit, yawn, swallow beer. Talk or sit silent. I am observed – the only white man in their haven. They look, but do not stare. There is no sense of hostility or accusation. We drink the same beer and the bottles keep coming. When the Castle runs out, we change to the more expensive Pilsner. An extra Z$10,000 per bottle – pennies to wet the dust.

A man sits listening to his opinionated colleague, the envelope in front of him marked 'urgent'. He orders another beer. They talk of politics and currency exchange. Their language swaps between Ndebele and English, as easily as the Welsh swap between English and Cymraeg.

The Exchange is wholesome. Honest. Like the Cambrian that sat on the corner of Cardiff's St Mary and Caroline Streets, before it became a shallow representation of Erin. I am at home here, just as I am at home in every bar in the world that serves as quiet refuge for man.

And I remember a framed photo of the President in every civic office, hallway and public room in the city. And I remember whomever I asked, however drunk I was or however drunk they were, nobody blamed anything on His Excellency. They could not. If anyone was to blame for anything, it was his ministers. No executive responsibility; never the man, himself.

Here in Brooklyn, only a block from the apartment I share with my wife often enough to be considered a local, I am sat in Moe's – a decent little dive that to its cost and mine is becoming increasingly fashionable as the surrounding neighbourhood becomes more gentrified. The guy sat next to me is still tapping his fingers, but no longer in time with the music. The vibration of his rhythm disturbs me. I feel it through the wood and along the bar and into my elbow. It does not reach the pain in my mouth or the pain in my neck – a pain born of standing upright and firm, of looking the world in the eye. Of walking tall, like a man, like the song says, all Mitchum-like. Doing so makes me ache. Far easier to bend like Aesop's reed in the wind; far harder to bend like Aesop's reed in the wind. Far easier to slouch at a bar all Mitchum-like and not stand at all. Far easier to crawl, if they must throw me out, and it's reaching that time.

When the Exchange eventually runs out of beer – as it does every night – I find my way to the Rainbow Hotel. When their beer runs out, I go to the bar across the road, then the beer garden, then the Alabama, then anywhere else I can find, avoiding as much as possible the attention of prostitutes who see this white man as easy money – a month's in a night – and quote their price by saying, 'My taxi home costs…'.

Here, in Brooklyn, the bars never run out of beer. Drink all you can and there'll still be more. But they can run out of welcome. And they can run out of attraction. And they can run out of character. And I can run out of money. And they can run me down or run me out and home.

The other night I walked through Bed-Stuy to the subway at Throop. It was dark. Not just the night, but the neighbourhood. As I strolled down Throop, a woman aged twenty, eighteen, twenty-three, shouted into her cell-phone and along the block about all these white motherfuckers moving into her neighbourhood. A fateful occasion. As she neared the end of her self-righteous statement, her racist and defensive proclamation, her eyes met mine, as I strolled all casual as if I owned the city, all Mitchum-like. And she faltered. She faltered big time. She was caught out; made to accept responsibility for her words, and she knew it. In that instant I could tell she didn't really believe what she was saying, but she was scared – just a scared little girl playing grown-up. Scared and so blamed others. Blamed the imaginary white motherfuckers like me, who just happened to be strolling down her street to the subway, as if owning the city, all Mitchum-like. I held her eyes. I demanded her eyes. I smiled. I was not friendly, I was not aggressive, I was not dominant – it was not a pleasant smile. But it was honest. I held her gaze and her voice gave out. She only found it again when I was two blocks down Throop and she felt brave enough again.

Bed-stuy is black. Bed-stuy is dark. Some in Bed-stuy are scared of outsiders. Presume the presence of enemy. I was not. Scared, or the enemy. Still, I strolled, all Mitchum-like, knowing somewheres in the night the young woman of twenty, eighteen, twenty-three, would find a quiet moment to question herself. She will not find answers. But the questions will be worth asking.

In Bulawayo, nobody treated me as an enemy. I was a white man walking; a white man drinking; a white man keeping himself to himself. No hassle, no demands, no expectation or friction.

In Bulawayo, the prostitutes swarmed around me like flies around shit. I was not flattered. I am poet first, and white man second. They had not considered how poets are the poorest, in any colour, of any race. And the richest. But a jewel-studded road is hard on the bones and sprains our ankles. Think what they like of me. I stroll from bar to bar, from Brooklyn to Wales to Bulawayo and back again, from brawl to wife's bed, and in my head is the glory of poetry. I stroll, get drunk, create, all Mitchum-like, and nothing like Mitchum at all. Let them think what they think of me. There are more important matters. I don't even care what I think of myself.

112

The guy on my left, who was drumming his fingers and sending vibrations up my arms and past my elbow but not far enough to drill my molars and remove the pain, has fallen asleep at the bar, and dropped his head on my shoulder. His sleepy presence weighs like a censor – ambivalent to look at, innocent even, but numbing and restrictive and constant.

I do not need an outside censor. The pen burns my fingers and I want to run from it. Rather, I want to stay here at the bar and throw the pen through the doorway into the cold night air and snow on the ground. Holding it sparks my arthritis and sears my being. There is too much to say. I do not know what will emerge, what will come out, what I will learn about myself.

I sit here with my beer and rum and hat on the bar all Mitchum-like, and pen in my hand. And I am sat here running from myself. It is time to stop. I hup and shake the weight of the drinker from my shoulder. Slide my beer glass along the wood of the bar, slowly into my other palm, so the left hand is free, so my left arm of power achieves some liberty. It is numb from the burden, prickly with newfound circulation. Within my left, the pen still burns; eases my fingers. My wedding band itches – uncomfortable with heat after so much cold; wary of the flow of the word, the soul.

The guy grumbles, tries to grab my hat. I push him back onto his stool and tell him he has one of his own. He cannot see it. It is on his head. I drink my beer. Grasp my pen and write. No one can censor except myself. No one can wear the hat, not even Mitchum. There are things to be said, things to be written, a different life to be led. So it is time to clear the tab. Time to get going. The pen moves faster than I can. And the present is here too soon.

THE SADZA EATERS
(after Van Gogh)

David Goodwin

A contemporary composition
Grouped in a lay-by;
Car-window-framed,
Frozen, by relative velocity

Into types. Their mute gestures,
Ordinary, no doubt, even profane,
Have become symbolic, grave with meaning.
Through the alienating pane

Sunlight glares away old-master gloom,
Yet the illusion of stillness, brief
And sharp, saddens all to a classical melancholy,
Implies a working knowledge of grief.

This sombre assembly,
Their worldlies done up with bits of twine,
Are retreating from my world
To one of thatch and thorn and kine.

Woman, bare feet planted on stubborn shale,
Her body's fruit swelling
By some hydroponic legerdemain,
Against hope, against all logic, feels the milk-sap rising.

SAFARI

Owen Sheers

Of the four brothels they visited that morning, Little Rose's Place was clearly the most organized. A metallic blue pick-up was parked at the foot of the stone steps leading up to the entrance. The truck had been pimped; black windows, thick tyres, chrome bumpers and an orange logo running the length of each side: *Bad Boyz Security*. Two men slouched in the cab. Another four sat in the open back. All of them wore sunglasses, thin vests, jeans and flip-flops. When Peter and Tiisetso got out of their own car and walked past the truck, six pairs of eyes followed them up the steps and into the lobby. Peter saw the barrel of a shotgun resting between the legs of the driver like the nose of a loyal dog dozing in the footwell.

They'd found the lobby itself empty other than for a woman standing in a barred-off kiosk against the far wall. A plastic sign tied to the bars told them to *Please leave bags and guns here*. Opposite the kiosk a pair of soundproofed double doors muffled a distant bass beat. Above these doors Peter could make out another sign in faded ochre paint, parts of its letters chipped away by peeling plaster: *Dress Code for all Customers is Smart Casual*. Directly facing them was a corkboard on which he noticed a printed sheet of paper pinned in the left hand corner: *Calling all Little Rose ladies – Meeting tonight with management. Agenda @ meeting.* Yes, Little Rose, whoever she was, obviously ran a very different place to the others they'd seen that morning.

It wasn't just these signs that eased the fear that had curdled within Peter for most of the morning. It was also the light; a flat white fluorescence from two humming strips on the ceiling reflected off the white linoleum tiles of the floor. There had been no signs in those other places. And there had been no light either, other than what scraps of sunlight made it through the few wire-laced, shit-smeared windows. Stepping in to each of those places off the bright Johannesburg streets, Peter had stepped into night. A night of shadows on shadows, flies tapping and buzzing at ankle level, and all of it wrapped in the heavy scents of piss and marijuana.

"I wouldn't call them brothels, as such." Tiisetso had said as they'd driven towards the first of these places. "Squats. That's all they are. Squats where the girls rent a room for a few weeks before moving on. New is good, so they always move on."

"Who from?" he'd asked her. "If it's a squat, who do they rent from?"

"Whoever owns them at the time. Someone always does. There's always a man taking the money. It changes."

Yes, Peter had thought, looking out at the passing streets of Hillbrow, it does. When had he first seen this part of town? Fifteen years ago? He'd come to a party soon after he'd arrived in the country. His first time in Africa. Twenty-five years old, smooth-faced and charged with an angry energy. Back then, standing in that lushly-furnished room, a glass of champagne in his hand, the party had felt like his first mission; infiltrating the enemy's headquarters, subversion from within. These elegant cliffs of houses they were passing now had then been home to the people he'd hated. Rich white South Africans, indulgent and arrogant in their mansion blocks on the hill. Living above it all. But he'd shaken them up, hadn't he? Both that night and with the pieces he'd written in the months afterwards, until the authorities caught up with him and sent him packing.

Tiisetso stopped at a set of lights. Two young men were washing a police car pulled up at the kerb. A blocky 1980s beat box on the pavement accompanied their wiping and brushing with a steady drum'n'bass percussion. Peter watched them, the energy with which they splashed the windscreen with a bucket of water before swiping it off again with their sponges in straight-arm arcs.

"They only come here to have their vehicles washed," Tiisetso said, tutting through her teeth and flicking her chin in the direction of the boys working over the patrol car's bonnet. "You won't see them here otherwise."

The lights changed and Tiisetso drove on, deeper into this place where, fifteen years ago, the chief of police's daughter had once lived, and where now the police wouldn't even show their faces after dark. Peter carried on looking out the window. They had all day. He didn't want to ask too many questions yet. So he just watched as they drove past the pavements, the cut-price shops, the street-sellers. Everyone they passed was a man. Tiisetso, driving beside him, had been the only woman he'd seen.

For a few moments they just stood in the lobby of Little Rose's Place doing nothing. Perhaps she's as relieved as me, Peter had thought. Relieved to have come across a bit of order after seeing so much chaos. He was breathing through his mouth to avoid scenting the air. The smell of that first place had made him gag. He'd felt the acid taste of vomit rise in his throat and he hadn't wanted to risk it again. Now, though, encouraged by the signs, the linoleum, even the pimped security truck outside, he took a breath through his nose. The smell was of pine-scented floor cleaner with a faint hint of spilt beer lurking beneath. He turned to Tiisetso.

"So, what's the plan?"

"The manager should be here to see us. He's been working with the centre. He even sponsored one girl. At the beginning. When we started."

She looked at her watch, walked over to the woman in the kiosk and spoke to her in Xhosa. She turned back to Peter.

"Stay here for a moment. I won't be long."

As she pushed through the double doors a brief wash of the music beyond flooded the lobby, diminishing again as the doors swung, first past each other and then closed.

It was the first time she'd left him all day. Obviously he'd been right to feel safer here. She was an impressive woman, this Tiisetso. The PR girl for the British NGO funding her project had said as much. Been one of these girls herself apparently; got caught up in it straight off the train, like so many of them. The tracks fed into the city from all over the country, bringing in a daily supply of new rural girls looking to make some money. Not that they'd had this in mind. Peter thought again of the rooms Tiisetso had shown him. How small they were. Small, dark and bare. A chequered mattress, maybe a bed. A single crucifix on an otherwise naked wall. Then he thought of the spaces from which so many of them would have come. The wide veld, the long plains, the broad hills. The comparison, the idea of this exchange of light for dark, rural for city, space for enclosure made him feel better about the piece he'd write on this. Not just because he was starting to see a shape to it, how it might work, but also because it reminded him he really cared about what was happening here. So he'd make sure it was a good one, a bloody good piece to shake them up, just as the ones he'd written fifteen years ago had. If he could find someone to take it. The usual editors he'd worked with in the past hadn't sounded too keen.

"AIDS in South Africa. Christ, Peter, where's the story? Hardly new, is it? What's the angle? Is there a date to hook it on?"

That's when he'd called the PR girl again and she'd told him about Tiisetso's own past. That had helped. The neatness of it. Reformed prostitute caring for the girls no one else will. And the fact it was working. Five thousand girls helped by the outreach programme. Seventy put through school last year. Working despite unhelpful statements from government ministers about beetroot and showers either curing or preventing HIV. It hadn't been enough to secure a commission but it was enough to muster sufficient interest for the NGO to risk flying him out. And God it had felt good to be back. It had been too long, that's what he'd told himself when he stepped off the plane and felt Africa again: felt her smack him in the face with her heat, felt her ease him down and rev him up, at one and the same time. When he'd taken a walk through the city at night and felt, once again, the purity of her rawness.

But then this morning, as Tiisetso had driven them to the first place, his spirit for it all had flagged again. He suspected he knew why, although he didn't like to admit it.

"Matt Damon, Madonna, I've shown them all around the project. Clinton's people have come to have a look too."

He'd nodded, raised his eyebrows to convey a suitable level of impression. Then asked the most aggressive question he could think of.

"But the infection rates are only dropping because so many are dying, isn't that right? And although the punters use condoms now, the girls' boyfriends won't. It's a bit of a losing battle isn't it?"

Tiisetso had flicked her eyes at the rear view mirror, indicated and taken a left turn. He thought she wasn't going to answer him, but half-way up the next street she'd simply said, "Don't worry, I'll show you something different. There were places I couldn't take them. There are just two of us."

They'd driven on to the first place in silence. He'd been angry at her for suggesting he was only interested in his story. That simply wasn't true. He badly wanted to write about what she was doing here, what she'd achieved. But not, he admitted to himself now, standing in the lobby of Little Rose's Place, as much as he wanted to be her, to have her impact, her access.

He wandered over to the notice board. There was little else on it other than the meeting flyer. A card for *Bad Boyz Security*, a missing persons' poster and another printed sheet giving details of Tiisetso's project. He looked into the barred kiosk but the woman had gone. He was entirely on his own. It was what he'd wanted all day, after the sheer terror of those other places, the menace of the streets and the cloying heat and sweat smell of other people. But now it was the last thing he wanted, so, giving one of the soundproof doors a hefty shove, he stepped into the room beyond.

Once again he had stepped into night. It took a moment for his eyes to adjust but when they did all he could see was the curved edge of a bar and a group of male heads silhouetted against the pink and blue sweeping lights of a disco. The music was louder than he'd expected, and not what he'd expected. *Time after Time* by Cyndi Lauper was stretching the speakers to their full capacity. He hadn't moved far from the door and, now he was inside, he didn't want to.

He must have felt her watching him, that's what he told himself afterwards. Why else would he have turned to look into that part of the room? It was unlit, a corner, nothing could have been there. Except of course, there had been. Her, leaning against the end of the bar's curve, arms folded, watching him. He took a step towards her and leaned in.

"Hello."

Maybe she hadn't heard him. The music was so loud and the expression of her face hadn't changed. He leant in again, feeling a little ridiculous.

"My name's Peter."

"Hello Peter."

Her voice didn't suit her body. She was fat. There was no other way of describing her. Her arms were fat, her neck was fat, and her jeans stretched over her stomach as taut as a sail in a full wind. But her voice was thin. Thin and quiet. And yet, unlike Peter, she didn't seem to have to shout for him to be able to hear her.

"And yours?" he asked.

"Rosebud." He nodded, smiling.

"And what do you do here, Rosebud?"

For the first time her face conveyed a connection. Raising both her eyebrows and her chin slightly, she cocked her head to one side. Peter thought he saw the ghost of a smile.

"I have sex with men for money. What are you doing here?"

Of course she does, Peter thought, it's a bloody brothel you idiot. Why had he thought she wouldn't? Was it her size? All the girls he'd seen today had been small, almost childlike. He smiled again, a tighter, close-lipped smile, and kept nodding.

"I'm a journalist. Do you know Tiisetso?"

She raised her eyebrows again, higher this time, to indicate she did.

"Well, I'm writing about her and her project."

Her eyes were looking straight into his but she was giving nothing else away.

"About the work she does."

The rest of the bar seemed to have melted into the lights and music. He glanced around and could just see smoke curling through the disco beams, vague shapes, but no other people. Turning back to Rosebud he tried again.

"Where are you from, Rosebud?"

For the first time she looked away from him. He felt as if she'd been judging him all this time and somehow he'd just failed. She didn't bother looking back when she answered.

"Botswana. I'm from Botswana."

"Ah, I know Botswana," he said, trying to pare the eagerness to please out of his voice. "I wrote a piece about the San, the Bushmen, a few years back."

Very slowly, she turned her head to look at him again.

"And what did you have to say about the San, Peter?" She said his name like it was a needle with which she was about to pierce him.

"Well, it was about how they were being treated, I suppose. About that fence that went up across their hunting grounds. The one all the migrating animals died against."

She was still looking at him. He waited, but again there was no response.

"The Botswana government weren't too happy about it. They banned me."

He paused again. She blinked and sighed, her chest held within her folded arms expanding and falling like a single wave long-grown over miles of ocean.

"Put my name on a list in an internal newsletter. Told me I wasn't welcome there again. Never been back since."

"Why are you here?"

After waiting for a response for so long, her question took him by surprise. She asked it as if he hadn't just been speaking to her at all.

"I told you, I'm a journalist, I'm writing–"

"Yes, I know. About Tiisetso. But why, Peter? Why have you come here to write about Tiisetso? To write about us?"

"It's important. An important story. She's doing important work." He heard himself and couldn't quite believe this was the answer he was giving, but it was true. That was why he was there. "People have got tired of AIDS stories, so any new ones are, well, important."

She smiled again, this time with a shake of the head.

"This is not a new story, Peter. It is the oldest story there is."

He didn't answer, just looked back at her, frowning.

"Where you are from, Peter, you have a house?"

"Yes, yes I do."

"And a wife?"

"No, I'm not married. I have a girlfriend."

"And she lives with you?"

"No, she has her own place."

"So you just see her when you want sex?"

"No! Christ, no. No. We see each other all the time."

She looked away again, into the lights and the smoke. Peter looked away as well. Where the hell was Tiisetso? She said she'd only be gone for a minute.

"So what do you think your writing will do?"

He turned back to look at her. The music was giving him a headache and he wished he'd stayed in the lobby.

"Do? Well, I hope it'll help, I suppose. In some way. Raise awareness."

"And will that make something happen, Peter? Will that make things better here?"

"Christ," he swept a hand over his face and through his hair. "I don't know. I hope so." He paused, then began nodding, slowly at first then more energetically, more to himself than to her. "Actually, yes, it will. I think if enough pieces are written, if enough attention is paid, something will happen. Yes."

She was still looking away, but now she turned back to him once more.

"Why don't you take me home with you?"

"Pardon?"

"If you want to make a difference. Take me to your country. Marry me. That will help."

He laughed. "Yes, I suppose it might. But only you."

"Isn't that something? Better than just maybe helping many?"

He looked into her face and realised she was serious. About something, if not about her proposal of marriage.

"Look," he said, glancing over his shoulder for Tiisetso again. "I should get going. I'm meant to be meeting the manager."

Now it was her turn to laugh. A short, breathy hiccup, but a laugh nonetheless. She looked away again, scanning her eyes over the room before bringing them back to rest on his.

"I think you are a good man, Peter. But I do not think you should be here. I do not think you understand."

She held his eye as she said this, and held it still in the music and smoke-filled silence between them afterwards.

What the hell did she mean? Don't understand? Peter felt an old anger rise in his chest the way the acid and bile had risen in his throat earlier. He'd seen those places this morning. He'd seen this whole area fifteen years ago. Christ, he'd been here during apartheid and then come back to cover its end. His writing had played a part then, hadn't it? Of course he bloody understood. More so than she did. He wasn't the one selling his body in a shithole like this. A shithole in a once beautiful area where they now celebrate New Year by throwing fridges out of the windows. Where the streets are empty of women and full of men on the prowl, the make, or both. A shithole like this full of girls with HIV who won't take their drugs because their ministers say all they need is a good meal or, even better, a quick shower after sex to stop them getting it in the first place. So yes, actually, he does understand. He does fucking understand. He understands that he was bloody delighted when apartheid died, but that something's gone wrong since. Something has gone very, very fucking wrong.

The butt of the shotgun hit him in his kidneys. He went down before he even realised he'd been hit, before he realised he'd been shouting at the top of his voice. Two pairs of large hands dragged him to his feet. He felt he was going to be sick. A man's face wearing sunglasses swam into view. And then she was there. Rosebud, prising the hands off him. Pushing him, no, leaning him against the bar. Her passive face suddenly animated with Xhosa. The hands went away. The sunglasses went away. The double doors opened and swung shut behind him, feeding thinner and thinner pages of light into the room. And then, from somewhere, there was Tiisetso.

"Oh, Peter. I'm sorry. I didn't know where you'd got to. Let's get you back to the hotel."

Now it was her hands, smaller, lighter, on his arm, leading him towards the double doors. He turned to look for Rosebud. He couldn't see her and yet, as they moved away from the dark corner, he heard her.

"Go home, Peter. Go home. And don't worry, I will stay here. Waiting for something to happen."

SIX PACK

Wame Molefhe

"Beware of six-pack."

Foreigners sound the warning. Men with sinewy muscles hear it and crawl into the ceilings of the mansions they build for the locals; others, who herd cattle in the blazing sun, hear it and move into thicker bush. Women, playing nanny to madams' brood as their own children grow motherless, hear it; they know not to venture beyond the boundary walls of their station.

Uniformed men begin Mission Clean Up, hunting in packs of six for illegal immigrants. Their mission is to flush them from their hiding places. Weaving through alleys, they search and pounce.

Freedom hears the code – too late. As she slithers under the bed, her door is flung open. Scrambling to her feet, she lunges for the red, white and blue plastic holdall Batswana call '*mozimbabwe*'. She runs but stumbles. Her sweat spills onto the floor: sanitary pads, cakes of blue soap and pills for her husband. Clinging onto what is left of her bag she plunges into the night, but black boots thunder after her. Muscled arms grab her and load her into the back of a *Landcruiser* and they drive to the local prison for her to await deportation to a motherland that has usurped her choices.

"Get out," barks the soldier. She climbs down and is herded into a pen, which holds her country-mates. One day, two days, go by. On the third, when the holding cells are full to bursting, the captives are loaded onto a truck. It belches thick, grey smoke into the air as it rumbles down the north-south highway. She sits next to a man, so close she breathes in what he breathes out. A stray elbow presses into her ribs and all the while the blistering sun beats down on them all. One man leaps off the moving truck and is swallowed by the bush.

At the border they are off-loaded. "All of you get out and don't come back again."

It's been a month since the Botswana truck deposited her and a hundred others at the border to their country. As she lies next to her husband she remembers when she first left Zimbabwe.

Armed with hope and her passport, she had taken what soaring inflation had left of their savings and boarded the bus for Botswana, the land of plenty. She did not know her exact destination; she simply trailed behind those who had made the trip before, and prayed that she would return before her ailing husband succumbed.

Using her savings, she paid for a place to rest. They slept, ten to a tin-walled room, packed like sardines. For a month she paced Gaborone's streets, ending up on the corner of White City, alongside her country-mates. All day she stood with her palm upturned, pleading with the drivers of cars that sped past to give her work.

"I can wash, clean, do anything," her eyes begged. She would do anything to earn money – except sell her body.

The day her money ran out, just as the moon appeared, a car crawled past the jobseekers. It stopped. The crowd raced towards it. The strong ones reached the driver before her. He rolled down his window a little; with a seasoned eye he sized them up, one by one, and singled her out.

"You – beautiful lips, get in." She hesitated, but hunger opened the car door and perched her on the leather seat. He parked in the bushes and steered her through the darkness to the pay-by-the-hour lodge where she had heard women's souls were stripped.

She entered the room and lay on the bed. The protest of bedsprings muffled the voices that chanted in her head: "Prostitute, prostitute." Her heels scratched his legs as he crushed his body against hers. Her skin looked tar-black against his brown; like the liquorice sweets her husband loved. She heard water splashing in the bucket as he cleansed himself of her, then silence.

A hollow remained in the bed where his body had shifted the lumps in the mattress. She sniffed the air. It smelt of illicit sex. She ran her fingers across the side table. Her hand returned with specks of dust, an empty condom wrapper and a 50 Pula note. She dressed, stuffed the money between her breasts and walked back to the corner to await another buyer. Her shame blended into the shadowy night.

She opens her eyes and finds her husband studying her face. He pulls her closer but she slides out of his embrace. "When you are better," she promises. The pills and food are healing him but the medicine is finished and the cupboards are now bare. She kisses his forehead, picks up her empty *mozimbabwe* and closes the door behind her.

Six-pack or not, she must return to Botswana.

SOME KIND OF MADNESS

Ignatius Mabasa

Has it ever happened to you? No, not what you are thinking. No, not even what Charles Mungoshi once said, that you leave home on your way to the pub, with the song *Sina Makosa* playing in your mind, and when you get to the pub, you find that very song being played on the juke box! No, that is not what I am asking.

What I want to know is, has it ever happened to you? That you leave the house on your way to work in the morning, but before you reach the gate, you get this strong feeling that you have forgotten something – something very important. You fumble in all your pockets and even check your wallet, only to discover that everything that you might have forgotten is there. Yet, the strong feeling that you have forgotten something continues to hang and weigh you down like a cast iron halo. You stand by the gate for a while, your mind rummaging through piles of rubbish in the mind dump, but nothing comes out of those efforts. You suddenly realise that you will end up late for work, so you tell yourself, "Whatever it is that I have forgotten, I don't care."

The other reason why you feel you have to go is because the woman from the neighbouring house has stopped sweeping her yard and is looking hard at you, as if you have turned into a pillar of salt. She seems oblivious to the fact that she is holding a broom and that she has a job to be done. Perhaps, in her mind, she thinks you have become mentally unhinged because you have been standing there for an age, with your mouth open wide, like a garbage can by the roadside. For her to think that you are still okay, you turn round and look back at the house, as if you were waiting for someone to bring you something. You lift your hand to give the impression that you want to check the time on your watch, but you quickly lower your hand when you realise that the last one you had got lost when you were drunk.

Wandering thoughts are killing me, haunting me. I drink to try to silence my mind, but the thoughts, like busy ants, run all over and torment me.

Now, my problem is this fat light-skinned woman from the neighbouring house. She is still looking at me, mesmerised, not moving. I have exposed my wandering mind to this fat woman, I feel like a man found squatting behind a bush, relieving himself. I quickly push the gate open and take long strides towards the road to town. At the road I start flagging down cars. My eyes notice something on the tarmac, a dead chameleon that looked as if it had been run over by many cars and had turned blue-black. For some reason, the chameleon cadaver reminds me of dried biltong. My mouth waters. It is small things like this that make me drift away. I think there are other people or spirits inside me that are piloting my life. I have lost control. Like now, my mind has embarked on one of its many journeys, leaving me behind, standing by the roadside, looking at this dead chameleon that has turned blue-black.

But who said a chameleon cannot be cooked and eaten? Roasted chameleon, fried chameleon, marinated chameleon, chameleon casserole. We need to be innovative and inventive. Did the old woman from Chivi not cook stones? Although the stones did not become tender with cooking, she served the soup from the stones. As for me, I would even try grass, lush green grass, not hay. Come up with grassburgers and grass sandwiches.

I am rude-awakened by the honking of a city-bound minibus. That is when I realise that I am standing in the road, looking at the decomposing chameleon that has turned blue-black. I raise my head to look in the direction of the honking, and I realise that the mini-bus is heading to exactly where I am standing. I don't move. It stops right in front of me, running over and squeezing black juice out of the chameleon corpse. I feel tears sting my eyes. My tears distort the dead chameleon into a cesspool of colours that spin and spin until I feel like throwing up. The minibus driver honks at me, and I come back to my senses.

I move towards the door of the minibus. Before I get inside, I look back and realise that the fat woman from the house next door is still looking at me, with her arms akimbo. She shakes her head. What is it with her? I lift my hand and make a rude gesture. She retaliates by sticking out her fat pink tongue in my direction. I am pushed inside the minibus by the conductor, "Hey *mudhara*, get in *manhi*, we haven't got all day for cat-shit!"

I get in and sit by the window. The fat woman is still standing, looking at the minibus – searching for me. I slide the window open and frown hard at her. I make such an effort to frown that it actually hurts my nose and eyes. I feel small drops of tears escape from my eyes because of the pressure I have exerted trying to conjure up the most horrible frown. The fat woman turns her fat hippo-behind and saunters back to where she had dropped her broom. I sigh. I am glad I have communicated through the frown. Why should she continue looking at me like that as if I have grown a tail and horns? Maybe I have? I raise my right hand to feel my head and check for horns. My heart skips when I feel a bump on the left side of my head. I let my hand drop.

I tell myself I don't care if she has noticed that I have spent a long time looking at a dead chameleon. It is not her chameleon, so why should she be worried?

The feeling that I have forgotten something returns, this time with a vengeance. I shake my head like one possessed, trying to shake off the feeling, but it is stubborn like a nightmare that re-screens itself twice in one night. The young woman sitting next to me steals a glance in my direction. I can tell she is trying to understand me. I peek at her ashen face. Her skin is too smooth, almost velvety. She is young. I try to smile at her, but she has not gotten over me shaking my head so violently as if to mix all the things science claims are in there – eyes, blood, brains, mucus, tongue. A cocktail. Then I sneeze. I sneeze again. Each sneeze very loud, spraying fine jets of mucus and saliva over those sitting around me. I feel another strong urge to sneeze violently, and my efforts to suppress it leave me with a mournful haggard look. I feel like I am putting on a heavy and hot *nyau* mask.

"Are you okay man?" one chap asks. I can tell he is asking not because he is concerned, but because he is annoyed.

I don't speak. I nod.

Then velvety skin sitting beside me shouts to the driver, "I think this man is going to vomit. Stop, I need to get off before he messes my dress."

"That is the problem with you people," the driver retorts. "You do not respect other people's offices. You want to puke in my bus and make it stink. Do you know what that means? It means I must go and park, clean up your vomit and buy an air-freshener, and all that costs me time. And, let me tell you," he continues, pulling off the road, "I will drop you here right now – the one who wants to puke and the one who thinks her dress will be messed, but you must still pay for the ride even though this is not your destination."

The kombi stops, raising a small cloud of dust. Everybody looks at me. I am lost. They are all talking to each other and not to me. My mind has sneaked out and is already home rummaging in the boxes behind the house hoping to find empty bottles to go and sell so that I can buy some beer.

"Why have we stopped?" I ask.

"I don't think he is going to be sick," says velvety skin, "I think he just needs psychiatric help."

"Then he is in the wrong place," says the driver. "This is not a hospital but a business. I need to get paid at the end of the day."

"Can we move on, I am going for a job interview and I can't afford to be listening to all this. If it is money you want, I will pay double the fare for that guy." A smartly dressed clean-shaven man shouts from the middle of the bus.

The driver violently engages first gear. The engine cuts. He curses. Starts it up again and furiously takes off. He raises a terrible cloud of dust that finds its way into the minibus and settles in a fine layer on our skins and clothes. The dust reminds me of my grandfather's dry fields. Then I see him, my grandfather. A scarecrow-like figure, talking to himself and poking his stunted rapoko crop. Then he looks at me and says, "Kutekenya, what happened to the land that the government redistributed? Was it all taken by the news-reader because he got the news first?"

I laugh at grandfather's thinking. I laugh loudly.

"I think this man needs help," a fat man in a tight jacket remarks, looking at me from the seat in front.

"But what have I done?" I ask innocently.

"Why are you laughing?"

"Has it become a crime in Zimbabwe to laugh? Amid all these shortages, where fuel, sugar, money, politics, women, soccer are all now a black-market affair, is one not allowed to laugh?" I ask, but I am not sure these are my words. They just oozed out. I didn't think of them. And I don't know if they make sense.

Oh, not again. That feeling is coming back. I look around me and everybody is looking at me, except the driver, but I suspect he is looking at me through the rear view mirror.

"Alright, I am laughing at my grandfather." I say, thinking people will understand me. It seems nobody does and I don't blame them because I don't even understand myself.

"But what is it really with this guy?" another man asks from the back seat.

"Too much *mbanje* and beer. *Kachasu chaiko. Kanopinda mumusoro*," an expert comments from another seat.

Velvety skin looks at me. She frowns.

"But it's not contagious!" I announce to the commuters, and to her in particular.

She frowns. I smile. Then I look at her eyes and I see my aunt in Chirumanzu. I left her at the big government hospital there in the dingy corridors that have paint peeling off the walls. The whole hospital had a hanging smell of amoxyllin that escorted one everywhere. I still see her as I left her, sitting with hunched shoulders in the ward next to her dying groaning daughter. That daughter of my aunt also used to have velvety skin, but now her skin is like old leather. She no longer talks or eats or blinks and is even shitting herself without apology.

Through the eyes of velvety skin, Aunt says to me "Kutekenya *mwana wehanzvadzi yangu*, death never used to be so sophisticated. Thandi is leaving me five mouths to feed, five bodies to clothe and raise, when I am a poor widow who is also knocking on heaven's door!"

I shake my head and say, "*Kwatiri kuenda kunotyisa tete.*"

"What is he saying now?" the man going for an interview asks.

"Something I don't understand and that I do not want to know or understand," velvety skin replies. She speaks in English in an accent that is groaning with effort.

The minibus veers sideways making me lean on velvety skin. She is too soft, spongy-like. She smells of cheap flea-market perfume. This time I feel I am going to vomit. I struggle to keep it in.

The minibus has lurched sideways because the driver is fastening his seat-belt as there is a roadblock along Seke Road near ABC Auctions. He slows as a thin, hungry-looking policeman flags him down.

"Looking for bribes so early!" the driver announces to the passengers, pulling off and stopping about a metre from the policeman. The officer looks like a scarecrow, a caricature. His uniform is old and the jersey has holes here and there.

He has a remarkable face. It reminds me of an obedient dog, yet there is something about him – something shifty.

He does not talk to the driver but starts going round and round the minibus like a miserable mangy dog chasing its tail.

The interview guy curses and grits his teeth.

The policeman walks up to the driver's side.

"Licence."

The driver hands it over.

"Permit." The driver hands it over.

"Now, follow me to the police car." The officer of the law walks over to his car, waving the permit and licence disc in the air like useless things.

The driver fights with his door. It opens and he follows the officer.

"Why have we stopped?" somebody on the backseat asks.

"What, are you blind? Can't you see we are at a roadblock?" the interview man shrieks.

"Actually I am blind," the man at the back responds, raising his walking stick.

There is silence in the kombi.

I break the silence. Without thinking, I laugh and quote from the Bible.

As he went along, he saw a man blind from birth. His disciples asked him, "Rabbi, who sinned, this man or his parents, that he was born blind?"

"Neither this man nor his parents sinned," said Jesus, "but this happened so that the work of God might be displayed in his life."

Almost everybody in the kombi looks at me. I smile.

"Who are you?" velvety skin speaks, clearing her throat.

"I don't know," I answer looking into her watery brown eyes. That's it, I realise with a start, that's what I have forgotten.

A STUDY IN BLUE

Deon Marcus

(for a closet Epicurean)

I wish I lived in a willow pattern
where, calm-serene, the shades of blue ask
no more than I could give or know; where all in time

the same remains, unaged, unwearied,
free as those two birds who only know of skies
clear of clouded sighs, or those three men who cross a

bridge without a fear, unplagued by
distant stars or unsure feet, while all's inheld by
a simple patterned band, that keeps without, and seals within.

STAMPEDE

Thabisani Ndlovu

Jekoniya heard the Great Leader's voice, its unmistakable anger troubling the roof of the indifferent winter sky, ordering him and his fellow soldiers to get all their weapons together and fight the enemies of the Great Leader. The ever-present righteous anger and menace were unmistakable as the voice urgently reminded them, just in case they had dared forget, that the enemies of the Great Leader were their enemies too. Enemies of the people. They had to be vigilant, the Great One's voice said – always watchful in this never ending war in peace time because the enemies of the people were mushrooming everywhere every day. The rest of his brigade were around somewhere, listening intently too. He could vaguely feel but not see them. How it had got to be like this, he didn't know. He was here and they were somewhere – close. Like your shadow when it falls behind and you just keep walking without looking back – knowing it is there. Like the Great Leader.

It struck Jekoniya, with a sense of panic, that instead of the three guns he had been given by the Great Leader, he had only one now. It was a rusty AK-47. How had it come to be so rusty? He couldn't remember. There were so many things that Jekoniya couldn't remember. Very strange, because a few weeks or months ago, he had been firing at some enemies in a war in another country not his own nor the Great Leader's. Did those enemies fire back? Or did he just pick them off like sitting ducks? At times it happened that way. Orders. Commander Senzo would not be happy with a rusty AK-47. Jekoniya knew he had to clean the gun. Anyway, he needed to get the other two guns. That much he was sure of. He had left them in his mother's hut. That much he could remember. The Great Leader had said he was happy with his soldiers who had just fought another war in another country – so happy he was giving each soldier three weapons to keep and use as they pleased. Jekoniya had selected three guns – a bazooka, an AK-47 and a... No. The third was not a gun. It was a grenade – a big one the size of the Great Leader's clenched fist. It couldn't fit into any of the pockets of his army uniform. He had carried it in his water bottle container. Somehow he had left the grenade and bazooka in his mother's kitchen hut. He couldn't really remember why. Because they were cumbersome to carry? Maybe he just preferred the AK. The AK had brought independence. It killed the white man.

He had to fetch the two weapons from his mother's kitchen, behind the crude wooden door made from the *umvagazi* tree. It had been made by Veza, the crippled village carpenter. Leafless trees stretched as far as Jekoniya's eyes could see – a nest of twisted limbs and gnarled fingers like a giant fishnet. He walked through the trees for three days and nights with only his instincts to direct him. He could see the solid door Veza had made, and behind it, his bazooka and big grenade, waiting patiently for him. He was surprised no one was stopping him. Not Commander Senzo, not the Great Leader. They must have known he was going to fetch his weapons from his mother's hut behind the strong door. They must have been proud to see him hurry away.

On the fourth morning, he stood on the edge of the homestead, realizing, for the first time, that he had a pus-filled wound on his right arm, on the very edge of the wrist and palm. He didn't care how it had happened. It was just there. Like the wind. Like the sun. There he stood wearing his military cap with earflaps, looking like a tired dog. Maybe if he removed it he would hear some sound of life? Nothing. Just hollow silence ringing in his ears.

The morning sun was a blood-red, muddied by winter clouds. The rest of the sky with its metallic grey covering of cloud looked lower than usual. Somewhat sullen, as if Jekoniya had just insulted it. The kind of malicious sky to spread pestilence. The kind of sky that would make him shoot his enemies with unrelenting vengeance. Where had that happened? In his head he heard the Great Leader tell him to hurry up. The battle was already reaching its climax and he, Jekoniya, had not fired a single shot yet. What did he have three weapons for?

As he shuffled toward his mother's hut in his big army boots, he noticed there was no smoke coiling out of the gap between the wall and thatch. There were no chickens scratching the ground for food. There was no smell of cow dung from the cattle pen. No mooing, no tinkling of bells. The kitchen door had fallen into the hut and termites were feasting on it. Yes, the sturdy *umvagazi* door had been reduced to paper thinness. The termites had also gleefully eaten their way up to the roof-thatch and made a big gap at the apex, eating away snake-like roads going down to meet the wall.

He stood in the middle of the hut. Light came through the roof like a spotlight and shone on his pimply face. His lower lip was cracking and blood seeped through. His tongue swept the blood into his mouth and, immediately, more blood rose through the cracks. The hearth had been deepened by rain pouring through the hole in the roof. Could this be repaired? He hoped for the smell of smoke-cured thatch but it didn't come, no matter how hard he sniffed the air. He sniffed the air until he became dizzy. Then it came, from inside him – the smell of several departures. Everybody had left. His mother, his two brothers and younger sister, Khethiwe. Where had they all gone? Ah, when he looked through the hole in the roof he saw footprints – six of them, cutting through the bush, disappearing into the Limpopo River and then… Now he could see only two pairs of footprints on the other side of the river. The other pair had disappeared, like his memory of his father. Were those Khethiwe's footsteps drowned by water? What about his mother's footsteps? He couldn't see them. The sun suddenly came through the clouds and shone too strongly into his eyes. He stopped peering through the hole in the roof. He lost the footprints and cursed under his breath.

There was nothing in the hut, not even a piece of broken pottery. Tufts of dry grass stuck out of the floor at the back of the hut. Maybe his mother was buried in that very same hut and her emaciated remains had nourished the grass in summer. Buried with her pots and her broken pieces of pottery, killed by hunger. The last time he had been home he had brought a lot of food. The Great Leader had given them food in the army. His mother had been on the brink of dying from starvation and found it difficult to swallow anything. They had forced her to drink watery porridge. When was he last here? Jekoniya could not remember. His pus-filled wound was now itching. He licked his lower lip again and tasted the saltiness of his blood. His stomach growled and for a second he thought he would fall down and never get up. As he gingerly scratched around the wound, the emptiness of the kitchen told him to look elsewhere for his bazooka and grenade. He should try the big house, built of brick and cement.

As soon as Jekoniya stepped out of the kitchen hut, the gaping absence of the house assailed him. It used to be right in front of the kitchen. He had paid for its construction. His mother had been proud of that big house. The only one of its kind and size in the whole village. The five-roomed house wasn't there any more. It must have vanished. Disappeared with his bazooka and grenade inside it. Wait a minute! Ah, that was it. His big grenade must have gone off and left not even one brick on top of another. Blown up everything into thin air. Blown up his education too. His mother had insisted that his certificate be gilt-framed and hung in the living room for all ignorant villagers to gawk at. "That is my son's degree. He worked day and night, reading huge books to get that," she would say to open-mouthed villagers. Every ignorant villager had come to see a degree on the wall. The gold paint glittered on cheap wood. The memory of that glow reminded Jekoniya of a secret sorrow, secret even from himself. He could not put his finger on it but it was there, like the big house that was no longer there. Maybe it had to do with why he had ended up in the army and brought home a big grenade that blew up everything, including his certificate. It was the sorrow of hunger. Yes, that was why he had joined the army. His gilt-framed certificate could not get him any job and the Great Leader was handing out food in the army. No. There was a greater sorrow. Something he had lost. Something buried in infinite folds of frustration and many years of shooting at many enemies that had eventually brought forgetfulness. Was his sorrow forgetfulness?

What was he going to say now about the missing bazooka and big grenade? Maybe if he fought hard again, he would be allowed three weapons. Life as a soldier was simple, Jekoniya thought, as he stared at the shimmering sand where the big house used to be. You pull a trigger, pull a pin and throw. Rat-tat-tat…boom! Finish. The Great Leader was waiting for him. The oily brilliance of the high noon winter sun said so. He didn't want to be the enemy of the Great Leader in this never ending war and this time he would keep the weapons on him. He would try to be less forgetful.

For four days and four nights (was it forty?) Jekoniya trudged back through the leafless trees, now and again stopping and scouring the sky for his mother's footprints. It could be her footprints were blown into thin air by his big grenade because, no matter how hard he squinted his eyes, he just couldn't see them. But he must not give up searching for them. He only stopped searching when he began feeling the presence of other soldiers.

"Don't worry about your bazooka and grenade," Commander Senzo said to Jekoniya on the fifth day (or fiftieth) when Jekoniya eventually rejoined his brigade. "You might not need any weapons, because there is a plan. So your rusty AK is okay." A plan? Jekoniya wanted to ask but the rain was spitting in a sad and cold winter way and he was tired. He soon forgot the mention of a plan. More cracks had appeared on his lower lip and the taste of his blood was that of thin soup without enough salt. His pus-filled wound had burst, leaving a gaping whitish hole. It must have been late afternoon. It felt like late afternoon – the grey sky, the faceless General and every faceless soldier. There were just the outlines of their faces and flat blanks where the features had been. So it must have been late afternoon. Had he also lost his face? It shouldn't have bothered Jekoniya – losing his face. But it did. His mother might not recognise him.

Commander Senzo was talking about the plan now. The plan, to abandon the Great Leader, not heed his call to fight his enemies. That way, the never ending war would end. "Let's all stay here," said the Commander through his absent mouth. No sooner had he said that than the Great Leader's voice, frenzied as ever, rattled the roof of the grey sky, "Those of you who didn't come to fight our enemies are in shit. My loyal soldiers are coming to wipe you off my land. You are desecrating it, this land we won by blood and have to preserve with blood." Jekoniya looked at the General's absent face. The General was quiet for a while before saying, "He's bluffing. He has less than a hundred men on his side. So let's…"

The ground thundered and shook. There were thousands of heavy footsteps approaching, with intent. Jekoniya's lungs quivered inside his chest from the stampede and he didn't need anyone to tell him to run. All the soldiers ran. Jekoniya needed to run faster than anyone. He had a rusty AK with not a single bullet in the magazine. It was useless and he flung it to the ground.

Jekoniya ran, darting and dodging among the leafless trees. Then suddenly, he was out of the trees and in open savannah with tall dry grass. He was bumping into many tough bodies. Bodies that fell down, got up and ran. Soldiers. Delinquent soldiers. Yes, he could make out their uniforms and guns. Maybe he should not have thrown away his gun. Maybe… Then Jekoniya started bumping into softer bodies. Some soft and small. Darkness was fast approaching and Jekoniya was now leaping and tripping over smaller and softer people who were crying. Once he thought his big boot had landed on the soft head of a newly born baby whose wailing stopped instantly. But he did not stop. If he did he would be knocked down and get trampled or, worse, the loyalists would find him still in his uniform, injured, and slowly cut him into pieces.

It ought to have been getting darker and darker but it was now getting lighter. Was it morning already or had the Great Leader found a gigantic light so the loyalists could pick out the dissenters? "Now my good soldiers can see you," bellowed the Great Leader. Jekoniya ran harder, realizing that he was no longer bumping into and tripping over any bodies. But his strength was draining. Above, the sky was getting angry. It became rain-dark but with enough light for the loyalists to pick out Jekoniya. The sky clapped and grumbled. Jekoniya's legs were getting heavier, his chest was on fire and his lips were openly bleeding.

The tall savannah grass gave way to a cracking-dry river-bed and Jekoniya collapsed onto it. He couldn't run anymore. The rain poured down furiously. People wearily ran past him – one here, one there. There was no more thunder to their footsteps. More and more people gathered on the river-bed. Through the slanting rain and spray of leaping soil particles close to his head, he could see their legs and feet growing dense, like the fishnet of leafless trees. Were these people as thirsty as he was? Waiting for the river-bed cracks to fill up and water to start collecting in pools? He wanted to shout that he was alive and that they should help him. But they had got the evil scent of his uniform and were moving away. They were not soldiers. He could feel that. It rained so madly but the cracks on the cracking-dry river-bed would not fill up. They were his pillow and would not fill up. Water just got swallowed into them and did not come up again. Not yet.

It would be a good idea to remove his army uniform and boots and underwear. Throw them away. His nakedness would save him. The scent of evil would go away and the people would save him. The loyalists would not identify him as a soldier who had refused to do the Great Leader's bidding. Yes, he should take off his uniform. But the uniform was wet and it clung to his body like a second skin. He managed to undo the buttons but the water seemed to have turned into glue. Jekoniya pulled and pulled hoping to remove or tear it to pieces, but nothing happened. Finally, out of breath and his muscles numb, he realised he didn't have any strength left, not even to break an egg. The madder the rain got, the more the uniform stuck to him and he could not reach the laces of his boots no matter how much he bent his body. Jekoniya tried to turn his head and face the sky. He did not have the energy. He wanted just a few drops of rain on his parched bleeding lips.

Someone turned Jekoniya face-up. He feared it was a loyalist and that he would feel the iciness of a sharp bayonet slide effortlessly between two ribs. But the hands were kind and, before he could look at the face, he knew the warmth was his mother's.

"Mother," he whispered, "I knew you would find me. Please take off my uniform before they kill me." With tears shining in her eyes, "Jeko," was all she said and her skeletal hands feverishly set to work, starting with the army boots and socks. As she gazed into his eyes for the second time, thinking she was through, Jekoniya whispered again, "And my underwear too." As she finished pulling it off, there was a roar of footsteps. "Run mother, I'm okay here. I'll just lie in the rain." She refused to move. The thunder of feet was almost upon them when Jekoniya found the strength to shout that she should run. She just held his hand and gazed into his eyes. Her hand was snatched out of his by the thunderous feet. Feet all over his body, hard army boots all over his body – tripping, trampling, stamping and stomping. Feet of thunder. His mother's withered body was being broken into pieces and trampled into the ground. He could hear her bones snapping like twigs. She was being buried by the feet of thunder in a river-bed whose cracks refused to fill with water. She would be buried under the dark clay and under water too, no trace of her footprints. River-weed would grow on her grave of dark clay under water.

The water was beginning to flow, lapping against his naked body that lay in a foetal position. Very soon he will be in water. He will be in water with his mother. In the water of his mother. Fewer feet were now splashing in water. Some feet were slipping on the clay. There was cursing and groaning. Some got up. Some just lay.

The thunder of feet stopped and Jekoniya listened to the absence of the thunder. The absence of the Great Leader's voice. There were no footsteps for a long time – all the time that he was listening to his heart beating reluctantly in a chest with ribs cracked all like shattered china. The water was now washing into his nostrils. In the stars of cough-choking, something became so clear that he laughed. Laughed bitterly. Was there anyone left with the Great Leader at all?

WHO KNOWS WHAT SEASON TOMORROW BRINGS

Gothataone Moeng

Every time he came back home with money and stories. Endless stories. Stories of his trips, the villages he went to and the people he met. How some of them, his regular customers, were almost his friends. He told stories of how the people looked forward to his arrival. How one solitary man holding a bag would be greeted with excitement. The children would go screaming to their mothers, "*MaZimbabwe!*"

The mothers would look up from their pots and, wiping their hands on their dresses, walk over to ask politely,

"Do you have any mangoes?"

"How much is your sugar-cane?"

"That green shirt would suit my little one," and the little one would smile, with head lowered, while still trying to look at him with big eyes.

There would be the usual banter of prices, the usual, "Ah, come on, my friend. I am just a poor woman."

The children would come with their bright shiny faces and their brown hands and ask for "*Manoko! Manoko!*"

And he would dip his hands into his peanut bag, because nobody could resist the children.

But although Tsitsi could identify the villages, she did not recognize the villagers from his stories. Because now one was even afraid to ask for a glass of water. The teenage boys jeeringly asked, "How is your President doing?" The teenage girls scrunched up their noses at the smell of your three days old

141

sweat, and the little children taunted with shouts of "We have no money" in broken Shona. Now the mothers savagely chased you from their houses. Just the previous morning, Tsitsi had been chased out by an angry woman from one yard. Tsitsi still could not understand what she could have done that warranted her brisk dismissal.

On that morning, Serwalo had just stepped outside the house to marvel at the mystery of winter in Serowe. She sighed as she remembered that the day before the sun had shone as if summer had already arrived. She remembered how the little kids had gleefully shrugged off their mothers' worries as well as their heavy winter jerseys and rushed off to play outside. Now she was mildly surprised to find that the slight spring rain she had heard was not just a fragment of her dream world.

"Well," she said quietly to herself, "who knows what season tomorrow brings?"

Retreating into the two-roomed house, she brought out a small blanket, and laid it on the verandah, then went back in for a little bundle of blankets in whose centre her son Tumelo lay snuggled. Kneeling on the floor, she made a repetitive clicking sound with her tongue and laid Tumelo down, then covered him with extra blankets. She moved the blankets up to his neck, smiling fondly.

Tumelo was a beautiful little boy, to his mothers' biased eye the most beautiful in the whole world. She kissed him tenderly on the forehead and stood up, her eyes still fixed on him.

Fetching her grass broom, she smiled gratefully at the imprints of the rainfall. The rain had done part of the job for her, she did not have to sprinkle the ground with water so as not to raise a lot of dust. Bending over, Serwalo swept with vigour, breathlessly singing the latest song. In her mind, she went over what she was going to do that day.

After sweeping, she would have to quickly wash the dishes from breakfast. Then she would have to find a polite kid to send to Merafhe's Butchery for some meat. Then, if Tumelo was still sleeping, she would quickly rinse off his nappies.

Facing away from the verandah, she heard Tumelo crying. Serwalo straightened up, abruptly dropping the broom and cursing at the slight pain in her back.

"Ijoo!" she screamed in fright, and then laughed in embarrassment at her fear.

"I am sorry, my friend." A woman of about her age stood in front of her smiling hesitantly. Her face was dark in complexion, and had two vertical marks dashing symmetrically under each eye. In her nondescript, loose fitting dress she looked clean except for the dust clinging to her ankles and liberally smearing her black *Bata* shoes. She clutched a large bulgy bag to her side, which she fingered almost fondly.

"I have something to sell, my friend," she said in Setswana.

Serwalo hurried to get her son who was now crying loudly and pushing off his blankets with tiny, clenched fists. She crouched down and reached for him, placing his face by her cheek so that their skins touched.

"Ssh, baby, what woke you up?" she asked, even though she had already made up her mind about the cause. Cradling Tumelo in her arms, she rocked to and fro on her feet. Turning back to the yard, she saw the woman waiting with a tentative smile on her face. Angered, she screamed in Setswana, "Get out, and go! Get out of here, you *mokwerekwere*."

Tsitsi did not understand the animosity in the other woman's voice, but when she heard the dreaded '*mokwerekwere*', she turned and walked away. When she looked back from the gate, the woman who had just hurled abuse at her was gently swaying from side to side, talking to the bundle within the blankets. She smiled slightly despite her sadness. Tsitsi regretted the fact that she and Goodwill had never had children, and now he was sick.

Goodwill was the man she had been living with for the past seven years. He had taken good care of Tsitsi when her parents could no longer afford to pay for her schooling. She had moved with him to Gweru, and she had worked with MaNdlovu – a stout and God-fearing seamstress. Goodwill still had his job as a labourer then, but went over into Botswana to sell a bit of this and that. Those were the times when he came back with his stories that she could no longer believe.

But now Goodwill was sick, and could no longer go out to work. He was the only reason that she kept going back to the yards of the people in this country. People who were black like them. People who ate sadza like them. People who used to survive solely on agriculture like them. People whose ancestors surely knew the unpredictability of the weather, and were subject to its impulsive mood swings. People whose lives were controlled by an invisible and invincible entity called government, which decided whether their lives were going to go well, just like them. People who, nonetheless, were unsympathetic, hostile and chased you out of their yards like you were not a person, like them.

From where she was standing, still trying to persuade her baby to go back to sleep, Serwalo could see the Zimbabwean woman walking on towards Mma-Nono's home. She clicked her tongue contemptuously; these Zimbabweans, everybody knew that they carried medicinal herbs, herbs that could harm her baby. Why was it that as soon as the Zimbabwean woman slunk into her yard her baby started crying; she must have something on her?

Serwalo quickly strapped Tumelo to her back. She was going to warn Mma-Nono. These Zimbabweans, one never knew with them, she was probably a thief as well.

She found the Zimbabwean woman kneeling on the ground futilely trying to talk to Nono's grandmother, who could not understand the Setswana she was trying to coax from her tongue.

"*Nkuku*," she burst in, "what is this woman saying? I just chased her from my yard."

"Serwalo *ngwanaka*," Mma-Modisaotsile responded, "what's wrong? Why are you coming in here and not even greeting us?"

Serwalo laughed self-consciously, and asked after the old woman's health. The Zimbabwean woman was still kneeling on the ground but now she stood up beating the drying mud from her knees.

She was getting ready to leave when Mma-Nono came out of the house. Serwalo started rapidly explaining that the Zimbabwean woman was probably hiding some herbs on her.

"As soon as she came in, Tumelo started crying and I chased her out. You should chase her out, she is probably a thief!"

"Serwalo," Mma-Modisaotsile said, "where are your manners? Your mother would be ashamed of you. Saying such horrible things about a woman you don't know."

"Nkuku, haven't you heard what they have been saying on the radio? These people are thieves," Serwalo insisted.

Tsitsi knew that they were talking about her. She could see by the way they were not looking her in the eye. She picked up the bag that she had put on the ground, and politely said goodbye. The old woman was the only one who replied, the other two women were still talking, about her. As she walked off she could see the old woman looking at her with sadness in her eyes, she felt grateful for the old woman's sympathy. She was one of the few people who had shown her kindness in this country, and she had learnt to be deeply grateful for a kind word, or a kind look.

Mma-Modisaotsile continued, "It's not in vain that our people say don't

144

laugh at one who has fallen."

Serwalo could not understand why Mma-Modisaotsile was defending the Zimbabwean woman. She remembered how just yesterday it was in the news that the Zimbabweans were crossing into Botswana, costing the government lots of money, money that could be used for other things. To her the Zimbabweans were a faceless mob of enemies intent on derailing what Botswana stood for.

"We are kind people, my child," Mma-Modisaotsile reasoned. "Don't let them say otherwise when they leave."

Serwalo was unconvinced, but she wanted to apologise to the Zimbabwean woman just to please Mma-Modisaotsile. Besides, she still had endless chores she had to attend to, looking after a family was no easy job, by God. When she turned to speak to her she saw the woman walking off. She had not heard her leave. She thought better about calling her back. She could recognise the pride in the way she walked with her back so straight.

VENDOR AND CHILD

John Eppel

Is that a shower of gold seeping
through gaps in the thatching of the sky?
What carefully wafting flakes are these
of light on fire, fading, to die

before they touch the woman and child
encamped beneath a municipal
cassia, now leafless, almost stripped
of life-transfusing bark? And when will

we halt beside her meagre tuckshop:
an upturned Lobels biscuit carton:
and buy a cigarette, a handful
of peanuts, and a blighted onion?

She cleared a space opposite the NO
STOPPING sign on Cecil Avenue,
a space she shares with sparrow weavers
bickering, and Matabele ants

that sting, and stink of formic acid,
with mandibles that nip the tendons
of her battered feet, and bear away,
piece by piece, the crumbs of her domain.

Sick, her child is the colour of ash,
a rag doll of hopelessness, symbol
of the new Zimbabwe. Who will buy
a soft tomato from me? Who will

deliver me from a government
of patronage, of cronyism;
a government of the obese, by
the obese, for the obese? Wallets

of flesh on the backs of their necks, folds
of fat behind their knees; like jumping
castles their bums, like teeming purses
their scrota. O who will deliver

us from these who have been coaxed into
temptation? And who will let that slow
light linger, those wafting flakes of fire,
and set the mother and her child aglow?

CONTRIBUTORS

Raisedon Baya (*Echoes of Silence*) is an award winning playwright and director whose works have toured internationally with Amakhosi Theatre, Rooftop Promotions, and Siyaya Arts. His plays include *Witnesses and Victims, Rags and Garbage, Madmen and Fools, Super Patriots and Morons* and *The Crocodile of Zambezi*. Raisedon writes a regular arts column for the *Sunday News* and has had his short stories published in magazines and anthologies.

Wim Boswinkel (*Justice*) was born in 1947, and is increasingly happy that he left his native Holland in 1970, to eventually live, since 1988, near Bulawayo with his family. Wim is now retiring from a lifelong career in farming and rural development work, and hopes to spend the next 25 years or so in tourism (including as a tourist) and, if the environment remains inspiring, writing. Wim's novel *Erina* was chosen as Best First Creative Book at the Zimbabwe Book Publishers Association awards.

Diana Charsley (*The Pencil Test*) is a Zimbabwean who's had several short stories published. She's keen on God and currently works for the Bulawayo Help Network.

Brian Chikwava (*Fiction*) is from Bulawayo, but has been resident in London for the past five years. He is a singer/songwriter and has released *Jacaranda Sketches* since arriving in the United Kingdom. Brian won the Caine Prize for African Writing in 2004 for his short story *Seventh Street Alchemy* in *Writing Still*. He was recently a Charles Pick fellow at the University of East Anglia. Brian's first novel *Harare North* is to be published in 2009.

Julius Chingono (*Bus Fare* and *My Country*) was born on a commercial farm in 1946, and has worked for most of his life on the mines as a blaster. He has had his poetry published in several anthologies of Shona poetry including *Nhetembo, Mabvumira eNhetembo* and *Gwenyambira*. His only novel, *Chipo Changu*, was published in 1978, an award-winning play, *Ruvimbo*, was published in 1980, and a collection of poetry and short stories, *Not Another Day*, in 2006. His poetry in English has also been published in South African and Zimbabwean anthologies.

Mathew Chokuwenga (*10 Lanigan Avenue*) owns and runs a clothing shop. As well as writing, he paints, sculpts and plays music. He won an award for English Literature in the UNDP Artists against Poverty Competition, has exhibited at the Delta and Verandah Galleries and has released his first musical CD.

148

Bhekilizwe Dube (Loving the Self) works as a literature teacher in Bulawayo. He studied literature, linguistics, Spanish and theatre arts at the University of Zimbabwe for two years. He has worked as a playwright, poet, dancer and actor with Sofika Performing Arts and as an arts administrator for the School of African Awareness in Bulawayo.

John Eppel (*The Awards Ceremony and Vendor and Child*) won the M-Net Prize in South Africa for his first novel, *D.G.G. Berry's The Great North Road*. His second novel, *Hatchings*, was chosen for the series in the *Times Literary Supplement* on the most significant books to have come out of Africa. His first book of poems, *Spoils of War*, won the Ingrid Jonker Prize. His other novels, *The Giraffe Man, The Curse of the Ripe Tomato* and *The Holy Innocents*, and his poetry anthologies *Sonata for Matabeleland, Selected Poems: 1965-1995* and *Songs My Country Taught Me* have received critical acclaim. His recent collections of short stories and poems are *The Caruso of Colleen Bawn and Other Short Writings* and *White Man Crawling*. His new novel, *The English Teacher*, is to be published soon.

Peter Finch (*Looking for the Southern Cross*) is a poet, critic, author and literary entrepreneur living in Cardiff, Wales. He is Chief Executive of *Academi*, the Welsh National Literature Promotion Agency and Society of Writers. As a writer he works in both traditional and experimental forms. He is best known for his declamatory poetry readings, his creative work based on his native city of Cardiff and his encyclopaedic knowledge of the UK poetry publishing scene. Peter has published more than 25 books of poetry, recently including *The Welsh Poems* and *Selected Later Poems*. Peter visited Bulawayo as part of a Wales Arts International/British Council cultural delegation in 2006.

Petina Gappah (*The Cracked, Pink Lips of Rosie's Bridegroom*) studied law at the Universities of Zimbabwe, Graz in Austria and Cambridge. Her short fiction has been published in literary journals and anthologies in Kenya, Nigeria, South Africa, Switzerland, the United Kingdom, the United States and Zimbabwe. In 2007, she came second in a SADC-wide short story competition judged by J.M. Coetzee and won first prize in the Mukuru *Laughing Now* competition. She lives in Geneva, Switzerland, with her son Kush, where she works as a lawyer for the ACWL, an organisation that advises developing countries on international trade law. Petina's first novel is to be published in 2009.

David Goodwin (*The Sadza Eaters*) was born in Bulawayo in 1958. He worked in private practice as a land surveyor until 1986 and lectured at the University of Zimbabwe until 2003, publishing some poetry in England along the way. He and his family then moved to New Zealand where he completed a PhD in customary land tenure, which necessitated three months of fieldwork in Zimbabwe in 2005. He now lectures at the University of Otago in Dunedin, and is still writing about Bulawayo.

Anne Simone Hutton (*Passing Villages*) was born in Germany and has lived in England, Zimbabwe and New Zealand, painting and writing. She is now returning to Europe only to be closer to Africa. Her work might not exist had she not lived in Bulawayo.

Monireh Jassat (*A Lazy Sunday Afternoon*) was born at Richard Morris Hospital, Bulawayo in 1970. A graduate of Rhodes University, South Africa she has devoted her life to the acquisition of knowledge and its distillation into wisdom. To this end she has travelled extensively, completed an array of courses and worked as a businessperson, clerk, librarian, paralegal, salesperson, secretary, teacher, theatre manager, waiter and reiki practitioner. All of which have paid the bills and provided background for her first love, writing. To date she has published newspaper articles, magazine features and book reviews. This is her first venture into the realm of short stories.

Ignatius Tirivangani Mabasa (*Prophecy* and *Poetry is...*) started off as a poet before venturing into prose. His poetry has been published in the anthologies *Tipeiwo Dariro* and *Muchinokoro Kunaka*. He has written two novels in Shona, *Mapenzi* (Fools) and *Ndafa Here?* His debut novel *Mapenzi* won first prize in the Zimbabwe Book Publishers' Association Awards in 2000 and was subsequently nominated as one of Zimbabwe's 75 Best Books of the century. His short stories have appeared in *Writing Now* and in *Short Writings from Bulawayo III*. He is married to Conelia and they have two sons.

Fungai Rufaro Machirori (*Rain in July*) is a young Zimbabwe-based writer and journalist. She holds a degree in Journalism and Media studies and has work experience as a media social commentator on gender and HIV and AIDS. In 2005, Fungai was the youngest Zimbabwean participant in the British Council Crossing Borders creative writing project. Her interests range from writing news articles, features and short stories to poetry. In future, she hopes to have more of her work published, and eventually venture into novel writing.

Judy Maposa (*First Rain*) was born in Bulawayo in 1972, and at an early age would lose herself in a world of words and imagination in the Tshabalala library. The eldest child of a family of seven she lived for some time in the early 80's in her rural Gwanda home, which nurtured a deep love for the open spaces and rocky heights of natural Zimbabwe. She is a former journalist and temporary Festival Co-ordinator of Intwasa Festival, but now has her own company, Art Connexion.

Deon Marcus (A *Study in Blue*) was born in Bulawayo in 1978. He has studied Accounting Science, Classical Studies and Ancient History, as well as piano and viola. Deon has had poems published in the three anthologies of *Short Writings from Bulawayo* and his collection of poetry, *Sonatas*, was launched at Intwasa 2005. *Sonatas* went on to win a National Arts Merit Award as well as the 2005 Zimbabwe Book Publishers Association Award for best poetry or drama.

Christopher Mlalazi (*King of Bums*) is a writer in the genres of prose, poetry, theatre and television drama. He has had short stories published in anthologies in Zimbabwe, South Africa and the United Kingdom, as well as on the web. He participated in the British Council Crossing Borders creative writing project in 2004 and, in 2005, attended the Caine Prize workshop. His short story *Broken Wings* was short-listed for the 2007 HSBC/SA PEN Literary Award. Chris is now studying for a degree to improve his understanding of the communication process. His first collection of short stories, *Dancing with Life*, has recently been published.

Gothataone Moeng (*Who Knows What Season Tomorrow Brings*) was born in 1984, in Serowe in Botswana, and is currently working as a journalist for the Botswana Daily News. As an aspiring filmmaker, she has worked in the production department for Precious Films, the production company making the No.1 Ladies Detective Agency, and has made a documentary film about the life of Bessie Head. Her short story *Singing in the Rain* won second prize at the inaugural British Council/Alexander McCall Smith short story writing competition in 2006.

Wame Molefhe (*Six Pack*) lives in Gaborone, Botswana. She has short stories published in *The Edinburgh Review* and *Riptide Journal*. She writes in between working, studying and mothering two children. She is writing a series of interlinked stories that examine life in Botswana. *Six Pack* was highly commended in the 2007 Commonwealth Short Story Competition.

Linda Msebele (*The Chicken Bus*) was born in Ntabazinduna, grew up and lives at Nkulumane, and works at the National Gallery of Zimbabwe in Bulawayo as an accounts clerk. Linda is also a visual artist, aiming to paint images of life and human condition through visual art, poetry and prose.

Mzana Mthimkhulu (*Not Slaves to Fashion*) was born at Mpilo Hospital, just across the street from Barbourfields stadium, home to Highlanders Football Club. At twenty, he conceded that his desire to play for Highlanders Under 19s was unrealistic and he turned his attention to the first team. Not having made it to the reserve side by the time he was thirty, he set his sights on the position of Head Coach. At forty, he almost made it to the position of sidekick to assistant coach. Never one to give up easily, he is currently gunning to chair the club. Whilst waiting for this inevitable appointment, Mzana kills time writing fiction and social commentaries and being a human resources practitioner.

Peter Ncube (*The First Lady's Yellow Shoes*) was born, lives and works in Zimbabwe, and he enjoys writing.

Thabisani Ndlovu (*Stampede*) was born in Lupane in 1971 and was educated in Bulawayo. He studied Literature in English to Masters level at the University of Zimbabwe and is now studying for a PhD at Wits University. He writes so that the reader takes an emotional journey charted by the words he puts together. There's a happiness in that journey, although some of the words talk of painful things. It is the journey that is important. He has won several prizes for his writing, the most recent being first prize in the Intwasa Arts Festival koBulawayo Short Story Competition.

Pathisa Nyathi (*And the Rains Came*) was born in Sankonjana, Kezi. After a career in education and public relations, he is now a cultural and historical consultant. Pathisa is a published poet, playwright, historian and biographer; his most recent publications include *In Search of Freedom: Masotsha Ndlovu, Material Culture of the AmaNdebele, Izibongo Lezangelo ZamaNdebele kaMzilikazi, Alvord Mabena: the Man and his Roots, Traditional Ceremonies of the AmaNdebele* and *Zimbabwe's Cultural Heritage*. He is a columnist for several newspapers and magazines, and is Chair of the Intwasa Arts Festival koBulawayo.

Andrew Pocock (*Hwange*) was born on 23 August 1955, in Trinidad, has lived and worked in Africa for several years and is an occasional poet.

John Simcoe Read (*Bababulele*) was born in Harare and has lived in Mashonaland and Midlands as part of farming communities. He trained in Pietermaritzburg, Cape Town and Oxford. While at the National University of Science and Technology in Bulawayo as Professor of Applied Biology and Biochemistry, he learnt a lot more about the culture, the history and the personal tragedies of Matabeleland. He recently joined the University of Botswana.

Bryony Rheam (*Miss Parker and the Tugboat*) was born in Kadoma in 1974. She went to school in Bulawayo, before moving to the UK where she obtained a BA and MA in English. She returned to Bulawayo after being away for over ten years, feeling a strong allegiance to it and to Matabeleland in general, but is now working in Zambia. Her first novel *This September Sun* is to be published soon.

Lloyd Robson (*Rum and Still Waters*) is a poet, novelist, broadcaster, workshop tutor, freelance book designer/typesetter and editor. Lloyd often works abroad and in recent years has worked in Australia, Europe, India, Japan, Sierra Leone and the USA. He divides his time between Cardiff and New York and leads a creative writing project in Sömmerda, Germany, every July. He has written commissioned documentary scripts for BBC Wales TV and BBC Radio Four. His most recent publication is *Oh Dad! A Search for Robert Mitchum*. Lloyd visited Zimbabwe to take part in the 2007 Intwasa Arts Festival in Bulawayo.

Ian Rowlands (*Innocence*) was born in Wales, where he still lives. He is a writer/director in theatre and television both in the Welsh and the English languages. His plays include *Blink, Blue Heron in the Womb* and the award winning *Marriage of Convenience*. Ian is currently a Lark Writer – one of the resident writers attached to the Lark Theatre, New York. In 2006 he visited Bulawayo as part of a Wales Arts International/British Council cultural delegation.

Owen Sheers (*Safari*) was born in Fiji in 1974 and brought up in South Wales. The winner of an Eric Gregory Award and the 1999 Vogue Young Writer's Award, his first collection of poetry, *The Blue Book* was short-listed for the Welsh Book of the Year and the Forward Prize Best 1st Collection. His debut prose work *The Dust Diaries*, a non-fiction narrative set in Zimbabwe, was short-listed for the Royal Society of Literature's Ondaatje Prize and won the Welsh Book of the Year 2005. In 2004 he was selected as one of the Poetry Book Society's 20 Next Generation Poets. Owen's second collection of poetry, *Skirrid Hill* won a 2006 Somerset Maugham Award. He is also a playwright and his first novel, *Resistance*, was published in 2007. *Safari* was written after his 2006 visit to Zimbabwe and South Africa.

Chaltone Tshabangu (*Pleasure*) began writing poetry in the early 1980s and took part in the then Bulawayo Eisteddford Society poetry competition. He has taken part in the British Council sponsored Crossing Borders creative writing project and has won the 2005 BBC Short Story competition as well as the Intwasa Arts Festival competition for 2007 and 2008. He is currently working on a collection of short stories.

Sandisile Tshuma (*Arrested Development*) was born, raised and lives in Bulawayo. She returned to the city after three years studying Chemical, Molecular and Cellular Sciences at the University of Cape Town, to study Development and Disaster Management at the National University of Science and Technology. She is very interested in 'third world' development and humanitarian issues and intends to pursue a career in international public health and save Africa!